The Modularity of Mind

AN ESSAY ON FACULTY PSYCHOLOGY

Jerry A. Fodor

A BRADFORD BOOK

The MIT Press, Cambridge, Massachusetts, and London, England

Eighth printing, 1993
Copyright © 1983 by
The Massachusetts Institute of Technology

Book design by Mary Mendell.
Jacket design by Richard Spencer.
Set in Palatino by The MIT Press Computergraphics Department.

Library of Congress Cataloging in Publication Data

Fodor, Jerry A.
  Modularity of mind.
  "A Bradford book."
  Bibliography: p.
  1. Cognition. I. Title.
BF311.F5615 1983   153   82-24892
ISBN 0-262-06084-1
ISBN 0-262-56025-9 (pbk.)

One curious feature about these formal faculties has yet to be mentioned. The doctrine loses every battle—so to speak—but always wins the war. It will bend to the slightest breath of criticism; but not the most violent storm can break it. The attacks made long ago . . . appeared to be irresistible; no serious defence was even attempted. Yet the sole permanent effect of these attacks was only to banish the word 'faculty', leaving the doctrine represented by this word to escape scot free.—C. Spearman, 1927

One day—it must have been five years or so ago—my friend, colleague, and sometime coauthor Merrill Garrett made what seems to me to be the deepest remark that I have yet heard about the psychological mechanisms that mediate the perception of speech. "What you have to remember about parsing," Merrill said, "is that basically it's a reflex." This work is, in effect, a sustained meditation on Merrill's insight, and is gratefully dedicated to him.

Contents

ACKNOWLEDGMENTS

This monograph started as some rather light-hearted lecture notes for a graduate course on contemporary cognitive theory that Noam Chomsky and I taught together in the fall of 1980. Scholarship is the process by which butterflies are transmuted into caterpillars—many drafts have flowed beneath the bridge since then. What has helped to make the process bearable is the generosity with which friends, relatives, colleagues, and occasional absolute strangers have chipped in with advice, criticism, encouragement, and useful information. I am deeply indebted to at least the following: Ned Block, Susan Block, William Brewer, Noam Chomsky, Daniel Dennett, Scott Fahlman, Howard Gardner, Henry Gleitman, Lila Gleitman, Michael Harnish, Peter Jusczyk, David Kaplan, Thomas Kuhn, Alvin Liberman, John Limber, John Marshall, William Marslen-Wilson, Robert Matthews, Ignatius Mattingly, Jacques Mehler, Mary Potter, Zenon Pylyshyn, Georges Rey, Brian Smith, and Lorraine Tyler. Special thanks to Jim Hodgson, who ran down references.

THE MODULARITY OF MIND

FACULTY PSYCHOLOGY is getting to be respectable again after centuries of hanging around with phrenologists and other dubious types. By faculty psychology I mean, roughly, the view that many fundamentally different kinds of psychological mechanisms must be postulated in order to explain the facts of mental life. Faculty psychology takes seriously the apparent heterogeneity of the mental and is impressed by such prima facie differences as between, say, sensation and perception, volition and cognition, learning and remembering, or language and thought. Since, according to faculty psychologists, the mental causation of behavior typically involves the simultaneous activity of a variety of distinct psychological mechanisms, the best research strategy would seem to be divide and conquer: first study the intrinsic characteristics of each of the presumed faculties, then study the ways in which they interact. Viewed from the faculty psychologist's perspective, overt, observable behavior is an interaction effect par excellence.

This monograph is about the current status of the faculty psychology program; not so much its evidential status (which I take to be, for the most part, an open question) as what the program is and where it does, and doesn't, seem natural to try to apply it. Specifically, I want to do the following things: (1) distinguish the general claim that there are psychological faculties from a particular version of that claim, which I shall call the *modularity thesis*; (2)

enumerate some of the properties that modular cognitive systems are likely to exhibit in virtue of their modularity; and (3) consider whether it is possible to formulate any plausible hypothesis about which mental processes are likely to be the modular ones. Toward the end of the discussion, I'll also try to do something by way of (4) disentangling the faculty/modularity issues from what I'll call the thesis of *Epistemic Boundedness*: the idea that there are endogenously determined constraints on the kinds of problems that human beings can solve, hence on the kinds of things that we can know.

I shall, throughout, limit my brief to the psychology of cognitive processes, that being the only kind of psychology that I know anything about. Even so, this is going to be a rather long and rambling story, a fault for which I apologize in advance. My excuse is that, though I think the revival of the faculty psychology program has been enormously helpful in widening the range of serious options for cognitive psychologists to pursue, and while I also think that some version of the modularity thesis is very likely to prove true, still the atmosphere in which recent discussions have taken place has been on the steamy side, and a number of claims have been run together that are—or so I'll argue—conceptually distinct and unequally plausible. Moreover, there is quite a lot of ground to cover. A proposed inventory of psychological faculties is tantamount to a theory of the structure of the mind. These are serious matters and call for due expatiation.

PART I
FOUR ACCOUNTS OF MENTAL STRUCTURE

Behavior is organized, but the organization of behavior is merely derivative; the structure of behavior stands to mental structure as an effect stands to its cause. So much is orthodox mentalist doctrine and will be assumed throughout the discussion on which we're now embarked: Canonical psychological explanations account for the organization of behavior by appealing to principles which, they allege, explicate the structure of the mind.

But whereof does the structure of the mind consist? Not, to be sure, the clearest of questions, but nonetheless a pregnant one. I propose, in this section, to consider faculty psychology as one sort of answer that this question can plausibly receive. (Strictly speaking, I shall regard it as *two* sorts of answer, as will presently emerge.) The primary object of this exercise is to delineate the character of faculty theorizing by contrasting it with several alternative accounts of the mind. My way of carving up these options departs, in some respects, from what I take to be standard, and perhaps the eccentricities will edify. Anyhow, I should say at the start that the positions about to be surveyed need not be understood as mutually exclusive. On the contrary, the view ultimately espoused will be, in a number of respects, quite shamelessly eclectic.

I.1. Neocartesianism: the structure of the mind viewed as the structure of knowledge

As practically everybody knows, Descartes' doctrine of innate ideas is with us again and is (especially under Chomsky's tutelage) explicitly construed as a theory about how the mind is (initially, intrinsically, genetically) structured into psychological faculties or "organs." I am inclined to view this Cartesian revival as very nearly an unmixed blessing. However, I think it is important to distinguish the Neocartesian sort of faculty psychology from other, rather different versions of the doctrine with which it is easily confused and whose rhetoric it has tended to appropriate. In fact, most of this essay will defend a notion of psychological faculty that is rather different from Chomsky's "mental organ" construct, and of which Descartes himself would quite probably have disapproved. The following discussion is by way of sorting out some of these strands.

In a nutshell, the central Neocartesian claim is that "intrinsic (psychological) structure is rich . . . and diverse" (Chomsky, 1980, p. 3). This view is contrasted with all forms of Empiricism, by which it is "assumed that development is uniform across (cognitive) domains, and that the intrinsic properties of the initial state (of the mind) are homogeneous and undifferentiated—an assumption found across a spectrum reaching from Skinner to Piaget (who differ on much else)" (ibid.). Issues about innateness will recur, in one or another aspect, through much of what follows. But, for now, I want to put them slightly to one side and try to see what notion of mental structure is operative in this Neocartesian style of psychological theorizing.

Chomsky likes to speak of mental structures on anatomical analogy to hearts, limbs, wings and so forth. "We may usefully think of the language faculty, the number faculty, and others as 'mental organs,' analogous to the heart or the visual system or the system of motor coordination and planning. There appears to be no clear demarcation line between physical organs, perceptual and motor systems and cognitive faculties in the respects in question" (ibid.). There is, of course, a point to this analogy. It rests largely in the contention (entirely plausible, in my view) that for mental faculties, as for bodily organs, ontogenetic development is to be viewed as the unfolding of an "intrinsically determined process." In particular: ". . . we take for granted that the organism does not learn to grow arms or to reach puberty. . . . When we turn to the mind and its products, the situation is not qualitatively different from what we find in the case of the body" (ibid., pp. 2–3). But though Chomsky's point is well taken, his terminology is in some respects misleading; important distinctions are obscured by a use of 'structure' that applies promiscuously to bodily organs and psychological faculties as Neocartesians construe the latter. It is, indeed, only when we insist upon these distinctions that we can see clearly what the Neocartesian account of mental structure actually amounts to.

It turns out, upon examination, that what Chomsky thinks is innate is primarily a certain *body of information*: the child is, so to speak, 'born knowing' certain facts about universal constraints on possible human languages. It is the integration of this innate knowledge with a corpus of 'primary linguistic data' (e.g., with the child's observations of utterances produced by adult members of its speech community) that explains the eventual assimilation of mature linguistic capacities.

It is, perhaps, not very important to this Neocartesian story that what is innate should be, strictly speaking, *knowledge*. After all, knowledge is—or so many philosophers tell us—inter alia a normative notion, having much to do with the satisfaction of standards of justification. Chomsky is himself quite prepared to give up the claim that the universal linguistic principles are innately *known* in favor of the explicitly neologistic (hence sanitized) claim that they are innately "cognized." (See, especially, op. cit., p. 9.) It *is*, however, important to the Neocartesian story that what is innately represented should constitute a bona fide object of propositional attitudes; what's innate must be the sort of thing that can be the value of a propositional variable in such schemas as 'x knows (/believes,/cognizes) that P'.

Here is why this is important. As previously remarked, it is the fate of the (presumed) innate information to interact with the child's primary linguistic data, and this interaction is assumed to be *computational*. Now, the notion of computation is intrinsically connected to such semantical concepts as implication, confirmation, and logical consequence. Specifically, a computation is a transformation of representations which respects these sorts of semantic relations. (See Fodor, 1975; Haugeland, 1981.) It is, however, a point of definition that such semantic relations hold only among the sorts of things to which propositional content can be ascribed; the sorts of things which can be said to *mean that* P. The idea that what is innate has propositional content is thus part and parcel of a certain view of the ontogeny of mental capacities—viz., that in cognitive development, what is endogenously given is computationally deployed.

So, Chomsky's account of language learning is the story of how innate endowment and perceptual experience interact *in virtue of their respective contents*: The child is viewed as using his primary linguistic data either to decide among the candidate grammars that an innately represented 'General Linguistic Theory' enumerates (Chomsky, 1965) or to 'calibrate' endogenous rule schemas by fixing parameter values that the innate endowment leaves unspecified (Chomsky, 1982). This sort of story makes perfectly good sense so long as what is innate is viewed as *having* propositional content: as expressing linguistic universals, or rule schemas, or whatever. But it makes no sense at all on the opposite assumption.

Seen from this perspective, it is perhaps the *differences* between endogenous psychological and anatomical 'structure' that appear most striking. It may be that the development of arms and the development of anaphora each critically involves the exploitation of a specific genetic endowment. And it may also be that what is innate can, in each case, be described as 'information' in the relatively uninteresting statistical sense that implies only nonrandomness. But there is, surely, no reason to suppose that the development of arms requires access to innately given *propositional contents*. There is nothing that growing arms requires one to cognize, innately or otherwise. By contrast, as we've seen, that propositions about anaphora (inter alia) are innately cognized is the very burden of Chomsky's plaint; ineliminably so, since it is precisely these innately cognized propositional contents that do the theoretical work in Chomsky's account of language development.

It is, I think, the essence of the Neocartesian style in psychology to assume that mental structure should be explicated largely by reference to the propositional contents of mental states. In this respect, no doubt, the new Cartesianism bears the imprint of Descartes' own largely epistemological concerns. Descartes was, after all, mainly interested in determining what sorts of things can be known, and with what degree of certainty. In his epistemology, the primary explicandum is our ability to recognize certain truths (of geometry, of theology, of metaphysics, or whatever); and the prototypical form of explanation is to exhibit these truths as identical to, or deducible from, propositions that are innately given and self-evident. Where the overriding motive is the explanation of propositional knowledge, it is perhaps hardly surprising that one should come to view mental structure largely in terms of the organization of propositional content.

I say that this strategy is prototypically Cartesian but, of course, it is on display as early as Plato's *Meno*, where the slave boy's ability to answer questions of geometry that Socrates puts to him is explained by reference to "opinions" that were always "somewhere in him."

SOCRATES: What do you think, Meno? Has he answered with any opinions that were not his own?

MENO: No, they were all his.

SOC: Yet he did not know, as we agreed a few minutes ago.

MENO: True.

SOC: But these opinions were somewhere in him, were they not?

MENO: Yes.

In Descartes and Plato, as in Chomsky, the nativism is so striking that one is likely to overlook a still deeper consensus: the idea that certain of the subject's cognitive capacities should be explained by reference to consequence relations (e.g., deductive relations) that hold among the propositions that the subject knows (believes, cognizes, or whatever). I say to you: "What's 2 plus 17?" and you, being good at that sort of thing, say "19." Your *behavior* is structured in the relevant sense; what sort of *mental* structure is the psychologist to posit in explaining your behavior? According to the Cartesian, it is inter alia the *deductive* structure of number theory to which the explanation must appeal. You know things about the numbers from which it follows that 2 plus 17 is 19, and this knowledge is somehow recruited—perhaps the deductions are literally drawn—when you answer the question. Similarly, according to generative linguistic theory, your ability to detect syntactic ambiguities, distinguish well-formedness from ungrammaticality, respond selectively to the noun-phrase that has been topicalized, and so forth are to be explained by reference to *what is entailed* by the grammar that you learned when you learned your language. In short, your linguistic capacities explain your verbal behavior, and are themselves explained by reference to the *content of your beliefs*. You can spot the ambiguity of 'they are flying planes' because, so the story goes, (i) You have learned the grammar of English, and (ii) it follows—deductively—from what you have learned that 'they are flying planes' has two well-formed parsings.

So, to return to ontogenetic issues, when Chomsky says that there is an innately specified "language organ," what he means is primarily that there are truths (about the structure of possible first languages) that human beings innately grasp. When he says that the mind of the child is "intrinsically structured," what he means is primarily that there are innately specified propositional contents. When he says that the theory of language learning is the story of how the language faculty matures, what he means is primarily that the ontogeny of linguistic capacities is the unfolding of the deductive consequences of the innate beliefs in interaction with a body of perceptual data. The moral: Chomsky really is a bona fide Cartesian in ways that go deeper than his nativism; the paradigm for mental structure, in Chomsky's theorizing as in Descartes', is the implicational structure of systems of semantically connected propositions.

There are aspects of mental organization for which Chomsky's version of the Cartesian story is, in my view, extremely persuasive. But, precisely for that reason, it is important to emphasize that there are other, quite different, sorts of things that a theorist may have in mind when he talks of endogenous psychological structures.

For example, consider memory. If one is going to postulate innately specified faculties, memory is, surely, a plausible candidate. Yet *memory isn't a faculty in the Neocartesian sense of that notion*. Having a memory isn't a matter of having one or another set of beliefs, and if memory is an innate capacity, that couldn't be because there is some set of propositions that organisms are born cognizing. There isn't, in short, the remotest temptation to identify the structure of memory with the inferential structure of a body of propositions. Memory is, so one supposes, some sort of *mechanism*, analogous to a hand or a liver or a heart. Viewed hypostatically at least, memory really does seem to be a kind of mental *organ* in ways that the putative language faculty, even viewed hypostatically, really does not.

The difference between these two notions of psychological faculty will be fundamental to much of what follows; perhaps an example will make the distinction clear. Suppose one believes the doctrine of George Miller's famous paper about the 'magical number seven' (Miller, 1956). Roughly, the idea is that there is a fairly constant limit on the number of unfamiliar, unrelated items that one can cope with in a task that demands immediate recall. (So, if I ask you to repeat a list of nonsense syllables, then the longest list you'll be able to manage on a first presentation will be on the order of seven items, give or take a bit.) Now, one can imagine a Neocartesian treatment of this phenomenon along the following lines: there is a certain mentally represented proposition to which one gives tacit assent—viz., the proposition that, when presented with a list of n things to learn, one should indeed learn the first seven and thereupon forget about the rest. (Perhaps this principle is not just cognized and adhered to, but also endogenously specified; for present purposes it doesn't matter.)

I said that it is possible to imagine a Neocartesian story that runs along those lines, but I doubt that any Neocartesian would take it seriously; and I'm sure that nobody else would. The sort of treatment that Miller's data cry out for is not the postulation of an innately cognized rule but rather of a psychological mechanism—a piece of hardware, one might say—whose structure somehow imposes limitations upon its capacities. To put it with all possible crudeness: the picture is that there's a box in your head and when you try to put more than seven things in it, some of the things start to fall out.

Perhaps it goes without saying that I'm not endorsing this picture; in fact, I'm not even committed to Miller's idea that there is an item-bounded short-term memory. The point is rather to emphasize a distinction between two quite different accounts of what mental structures—endogenous or otherwise—might be like; one account elaborated around a notion of propositional content and the other around the notion of a psychological mechanism. The former view of mental structure is typically Neocartesian; the latter, however, is not.

I remarked at the outset that the various notions of faculty psychology that I'll be reviewing aren't necessarily mutually exclusive. A Neocartesian could—in my view, a Neocartesian *should*—perfectly well take the line that mental-organs-qua-propositional-structures are only part of the story that faculty psychologists have to tell, much of the rest of the story being involved with the postulation of mental mechanisms. Indeed, it's hard to see how this suggestion could reasonably be resisted. That you say "19" when I say "7 + 12, please" is, no doubt, partly to be explained by reference to what you know about the numbers. But there must be more to it since, after all, knowledge doesn't eventuate in behavior in virtue of its propositional content alone. It seems obvious that you need mechanisms to put what you know into action; mechanisms that function to bring the organization of behavior into conformity with the propositional structures that are cognized. This is the problem of 'performance' in one of Chomsky's uses of that notion. Performance mechanisms do for Chomsky some of what the pineal gland was supposed to do for Descartes: they are invoked to answer the question "How does the structure of behavior come to mirror the propositional structures that one cognizes?"

Equally pressing for a Cartesian, however, is a subtler and prior question—one which I think Descartes himself never faced—viz., "How does the structure of *thought* come to mirror propositional structure?" According to the Cartesian account, you can figure out that 7 plus 12 equals 19 because you know things about the numbers from which it follows that 7 plus 12 equals 19. But, surely, this explanation is an enthymeme; it must be short for something like "You can figure out . . . because it follows from what you know about the numbers *and you have some way of figuring out* (some of) *what follows from what you know about the numbers.*"

In short, even assuming the Cartesian story about endogenously cognized propositions, we need answers for questions of the form: "Given that so and so entails such and such, in virtue of what psychological mechanisms is the organism able to infer from cognizings of so and so to cognizings of such and such?" Psychological faculties may well be invoked to answer this sort of question; faculties which mediate, for example, the representation, retention, retrieval, and inferential elaboration of the cognized propositions. These faculties—patently *not* mental organs as Neocartesians understand that notion—would nevertheless count as bona fide mental structures and might well themselves be innately specified (or, if they are not, then their ontogeny has to be accounted for, just as the ontogeny of propositional knowledge does). The point is, once again, that this sort of mental structure does not consist in the internal representation of propositions, and a nativism of such structures would not be a theory of innate *beliefs*. The Neocartesian appropriation of the terminology of mental faculties, organs, and mechanisms to express what is, in fact, a nativism of propositional attitudes tends to obscure this difference; but alertness to it is essential to understanding the range of options available for theory construction in cognitive science.[1]

I.2.   Mental structure as functional architecture: horizontal faculties

We turn, then, to a different notion of mental structure, one according to which a psychological faculty is par excellence a sort of mechanism. Neocartesians individuate faculties by reference to their typical propositional contents (so that, for example, the putative language organ is so identified in virtue of the information about linguistic universals that it contains). By contrast, according to the present account, a faculty is individuated *by reference to its typical effects*, which is to say that it is functionally individuated. If there is a language faculty in this sense of faculty, then it is whatever piece of (presumably neurological) machinery functions to mediate the assimilation and employment of verbal capacities.

One way to appreciate this distinction between faculties-cum-belief-structures and faculties-cum-psychological-mechanisms is to notice that even theorists who are blatantly Empiricist in respect of the former may nevertheless be (anyhow, closet) Nativists in respect of the latter. This was, in fact, John Locke's position according to some authorities.

> . . . Locke thought too obvious to mention explicitly in the *Essay* . . . the existence of natural faculties such as perception, understanding and memory, and innate mental powers like those of abstraction, comparison and discernment. The 'white paper' metaphor is meant to indicate that the understanding (and hence the mind) is originally empty of *objects* of thought like ideas; but it has whatever apparatus is necessary to acquire them through experience, and then to derive knowledge by comparing and contrasting them with each other.[2] [Harris, 1977]

So, then, the (noncartesian) faculty psychologist is per se interested in the analysis of mind into interacting component mechanisms.[3] However, the history of this kind of faculty psychology exhibits two variants of the doctrine according to the axis along which the mind is sliced. According to the most familiar version—which I shall call 'horizontal' faculty psychology—cognitive processes exhibit the interaction of such faculties as, e.g., memory, imagination, attention, sensibility, perception, and so forth; and the character of each such process is determined by the particular mix of faculties that it recruits. However, the character of mentation is more or less *in*dependent of its subject matter; the faculties are supposed to be invariant from one topic of thought to the next.[4]

For example, traditional accounts of the mind often acknowledged a faculty of *judgment*, whose characteristic function was supposed to be the recognition of identities and differences among mental contents (in one terminology among Ideas). A very refined judgment is one which can distinguish between even very similar Ideas (in the manner, say, of John Austin distinguishing a mere accident from a full-blooded inadvertence). Judgment found work to do in (e.g.) perceptual recognition, where the categorization of current sensory data is supposed to require comparing it with information from memory; but the details needn't concern us here.

Now, this faculty of judgment might get exercised in respect of matters aesthetic, legal, scientific, practical, or moral, and this list is by no means exhaustive. The point is that, according to the horizontal treatment of mental structure, *it is the self-same faculty of judgment every time.* The discrimination of identity and difference among aesthetic ideas is thus performed by precisely the same psychological mechanism that distinguishes, as it might be, weight from mass or torts from misdemeanors. On this view, then, aesthetic judgment is simply the application of the faculty of judgment to the process of drawing aesthetic distinctions. It follows that there is no such thing as a faculty-of-aesthetic-judgment per se. A fortiori, there is no such thing as an aesthetic faculty.

Or consider memory again. A recurrent theme in the traditional literature is the treatment of memory as a *place* where beliefs are stored. Plato has it at one point in the *Theatetus* that memory is like a birdcage; one, as it were, reaches in and pulls out the thing recalled:

SOCRATES: . . . let us suppose that every mind contains a kind of aviary stocked with birds of every sort, some in flocks apart, some in small groups, and some solitary, flying among them all.

THEATETUS: Be it so. What follows?

SOC: When we are babies, we must suppose this receptacle empty, and take the birds to stand for pieces of knowledge. Whenever a person acquires any piece of knowledge and shuts it up in his enclosure, we may say he has learned or discovered the thing of which this is the knowledge, and that is what "knowing" means.

THE: Be it so.

SOC: Now think of him hunting once more for any piece of knowledge that he wants, catching, holding it, and letting it go again.

This sort of architectural analogy is quite characteristic of faculty psychologies in general. The mind has an intrinsic structure, and mental contents have instantaneous locations with respect to this enduring background; things happen *in* the mind, and what can happen is constrained by the character of the mental layout.[5]

What makes Plato's story about memory a version of *horizontal* faculty psychology, however, is his view about how the birds are kept. The crucial point is that all the memories are in the same place. Or if, as many modern theories would have it, there are *several* memory systems, all horizontal faculties, then presumably each memory may pass through every such system. More precisely, where a given memory is at a given instant depends, perhaps, on how much time has elapsed, or on how much rehearsal there has been. But what it does *not* depend upon is the *content* of the memory. For example, there could not, in point of definition, be a *horizontal* faculty that is specific to remembering 'events' as opposed to remembering 'propositions', or to remembering faces as opposed to remembering tunes. By definition, such content-specific faculties would fail to be horizontal.

As remarked above, more evolved forms of faculty psychology than Plato's tend to think of mental architecture as, at least in the first instance, functional rather than literally spatial. A memory system is thus individuated by reference to its characteristic operations, it being left open whether there are distinct areas of the brain that are specific to the functions that the system carries out. However, the idea of a horizontal faculty survives the abandonment of spatial principles of individuation in favor of functional ones. Instead of speaking of the *location* of a mental content at time t, one speaks of the set of mental processes that have access to that content at t—roughly, the set of processes for which it constitutes a domain at t. So, a content that is 'in' short-term memory (but not in long-term memory) at 2:35 on the morning of the 5th is one to which short-term memory processes (but not long-term ones) have access at that date and time. A thoroughly horizontal faculty, functionally individuated, is thus one to which *every* mental content may be accessible at one time or other. Probably nobody believes that there really are horizontal faculties in that very strong sense, but the idealization establishes a useful point of reference.

That's about all that I propose to say about horizontal faculties just now. The character of the construct will emerge in contrast with alternative theoretical options. For present purposes, a horizontal faculty is a functionally distinguishable cognitive system whose operations cross content domains. I shall assume without argument that mental processes are computational insofar as they are cognitive, hence that the typical function of cognitive mechanisms is the transformation of mental representations (see Fodor, 1975). It follows that each distinct cognitive faculty must effect a characteristic pattern of such transformations. I shall also assume that we can make some sense of individuating content domains independent of the individuation of cognitive faculties, since if we cannot the question whether the operation of such faculties cross content domains doesn't arise. I suppose this latter assumption to be not unreasonable. If, for example, there is some psychological mechanism that is engaged both in the identification of wildflowers and in the balancing of one's checkbook, then we have, prima facie, good reason to suppose that mechanism to be horizontal.

I.3. Mental structure as functional architecture: vertical faculties

Horizontal faculty psychology has been with us always; it seems to be the common-sense theory of the mind. By contrast, the 'vertical' tradition in faculty psychology has specifiable historical roots. It traces back to the work of Franz Joseph Gall (1758–1828), the founding father of phrenology and a man who appears to have had an unfairly rotten press.

According to Gall, the traditional census of horizontal mental faculties is largely a fiction. There is, in particular, no such thing as judgment, no such thing as attention, no such thing as volition, no such thing as memory; in fact, there are no horizontal faculties at all. Instead, there is a bundle of what Gall variously describes as propensities, dispositions, qualities, aptitudes, and fundamental powers; of these an aptitude for music will do as an example. (I should emphasize that Gall does *not* himself speak of 'vertical faculties'. I have coined that term to suggest a certain reading of Gall's text—viz., that he agrees with traditional faculty theories that the mind is structured into functionally distinguishable subsystems, but disagrees about how the divisions between these systems should be drawn.)

From the point of view of a modern cognitive psychologist, Gall's aptitudes constitute something of a mixed bag. Indeed, there is a sense in which aptitudes are a mixed bag from *anybody's* point of view, since the term applies indiscriminately to both *competences* and *proclivities*. An aptitude to commit murder (to mention another of Gall's examples) is a propensity rather than a talent; you're apt to commit murder if you're inclined to kill, however clumsily you carry out your homicides. Compare an aptitude for music, which one lacks unless one is *good at*—not just inclined toward—things musical. This slight tendency of the concept of an aptitude to misbehave may have misled Gall into thinking that his vertical faculties have more in common than in fact they do. Certainly the census of vertical faculties that Gall acknowledges pays less attention to the distinction between cognition and volition than most theorists now believe to be proper.

Anyhow, in the case of what Gall sometimes calls the "intellectual" capacities, it is useful to identify an aptitude with competence in a certain cognitive domain; in which case, the intellectual aptitudes (unlike, n.b., the horizontal faculties) are distinguished by reference to their subject matter. It is of central importance to understand that, in thus insisting upon domain specificity, Gall is not simply making the conceptual point that if music (e.g.) is distinct from mathematics, then musical aptitude is correspondingly distinct from mathematical aptitude. Gall is also claiming that the psychological mechanisms which subserve the one capacity are different, de facto, from those that subserve the other. I take it that this claim is the heart of Gall's theory.

In fact, some of Gall's favorite analogies for aptitudes are ethological. Nest-building and bird song are presumably not to be viewed as applications of a general intellectual capacity to the accomplishment of specific ends; it would thus be a mistake to postulate a horizontal faculty of avian intellect of which competence in singing and nesting are among the manifestations. Similarly with man: "There are as many different kinds of intellect as there are distinct qualities. . . . One individual may have considerable intellect relative to one fundamental power, but a very narrow one in reference to every other. . . . A special faculty of intellect or understanding is as entirely inadmissible as a special faculty of instinct" (p. 240) (all Gall quotations are from Hollander, 1920). Intellect per se could not, therefore, be neurologically localizable, any more than instinct per se could be subserved by a specific brain mechanism.

Gall's point is precisely analogous to one that could be made by denying that there is such a thing as *acuity*. There are, no doubt, visual acuity, auditory acuity, and perhaps gustatory and intellectual acuity as well. And one might add that a given individual may have considerable acuity relative to one fundamental power, but very narrow acuity in reference to every other. However, since visual, auditory, gustatory, and intellectual acuity are surely just parameters of vision, audition, taste, and intellect respectively, it follows that there could be no such things as a *faculty of acuity*; that would be the wrong way to carve things up. Acuity, to put it in trendy terms, is syncategoramatic; and so, for Gall, is intellect.

Moreover, what is true of intellect and acuity is also true of memory, judgment, volition, attention, and the rest of the horizontal faculties; on Gall's account they are, one and all, the spectral progeny of misplaced concreteness. "Perception and memory are only attributes common to the fundamental psychological qualities, but not faculties in themselves; and consequently they can have no proper centers in the brain" (p. 240). In this respect, the horizontal faculties, which Gall denigrates, are explicitly contrasted with the vertical faculties, which he endorses; the latter correspond to specific brain mechanisms which Gall hoped, sooner or later, to locate:

Take the musician. He would not be a musician if he did not *perceive* the relation of tones, if he had no *memory* of music, if he could not judge of melody and harmony.... Thus attention, perception, memory, judgment and imagination are nothing else than different modes of action of every one of the fundamental capacities. When the primary mental power is energetic so will these attributes be; when it is feebly developed, there will be a feeble degree of attention, of perception, of memory, a defective judgment and no imagination.... We have to discover the fundamental powers of the mind, for it is only these that can have separate organs in the brain. [p. 238]

It is perhaps not surprising, since Gall emphasizes the specificity of the neural mechanisms which subserve the vertical faculties, that he should infer from neural specificity that there is what we would call genetic determination:

The influence of education, instruction, example and of surrounding circumstances acts principally when the innate dispositions are neither too feeble nor too energetic.... The impressions received through our senses from external sources are not the origins of our aptitudes, talents, sentiments, instincts and propensities.... The propensities and instincts, the aptitudes and talents, the intellectual abilities and moral qualities of men and animals are innate. [pp. 250–251]

This style of theorizing, combining nativism with an emphasis upon the domain specificity of cognitive capacities, will seem familiar to those who have been exposed to what John Marshall calls the "new organology."[6]

Much of what follows in this section will be concerned with the elaboration of Gall's vertical faculty idea, since it seems to me that there is much in this notion that modern cognitive science would do well to ponder. First, however, Gall's positive proposals need to be disentangled from a couple of arguments which he thinks show that horizontal versions of faculty psychology must be seriously defective. These arguments were portentous; they go rumbling down the history of psychology, repeated again and again (usually without citation of their source). However, despite their influence in reinforcing the antifaculty bias in much modern psychological theorizing, they actually aren't very convincing.

Gall's major argument against horizontal faculties turns on the idea that if there is only *one* faculty of (say) memory, then if somebody is good at remembering *any* sort of thing, he ought to be good at remembering *every* sort of thing. That is, Gall thinks the existence of a unitary horizontal faculty of memory would imply that an individual's capacity for recalling things ought to be highly correlated across kinds of tasks (across what I have been calling cognitive domains). Similarly, mutatis mutandis, for judgment, imagination, attention, and the rest. "If perception and memory were fundamental forces, there would be no reason why they should be manifested so very differently, according as they are exercised on different objects. There would be no reason why the same, and, in fact, every individual, should not learn geometry, music, mechanics and arithmetic, with equal facility since their memory would be equally faithful for all these things" (pp. 240–241). This is, perhaps, supposed to be a sort of 'Leibnitz' Law' argument: the same faculty cannot be both weak and strong, so if it sometimes happens that mathematical memory is weak and musical memory robust, then the memory that mediates mathematics can't be the same as the memory that mediates music.

If, however, that *is* the argument, it is clearly fallacious. All that can be inferred, strictly speaking, is that mathematical memory ≠ musical memory; which, though patently true, is quite compatible with mathematical memory and musical memory being exercises of the self-same faculty with respect to mathematics in the one case and music in the other. To put the point slightly less ponderously: there is no obvious reason why the same faculty should not be strong in one employment and weak in another, so long as the employments are not themselves identical.

It would thus be open to a faculty psychologist of the horizontal persuasion to suggest that what is characteristic of each mental capacity is the specific mix of horizontal faculties that it recruits, and to explain the unequal distribution of, e.g., memory across cognitive domains by reference to the interaction effects that different mixes of faculties give rise to. It now seems clear, for example, that the fact that top-level chess players remember distributions of chess pieces better than they remember other sorts of things does *not* warrant the conclusion that there is a specific memory for chess. On the contrary, it turns out that the operative principle is that, quite generally, one remembers what one understands. (Bartlett, 1932; Bransford, Barclay, and Franks, 1972.) The chess player's ability to remember where the pieces are is thus part and parcel of his grasp of how they might have got there. Witness the fact that it disappears when the pieces are set down in ways that don't make sense (DeGroot, 1965). Spearman (1927, pp. 35–36) remarks that the 'problem of correlation'—in effect, the interaction of the level of functioning of a faculty with the cognitive domain in which it is employed—is the insuperable difficulty for horizontal versions of faculty psychology: " . . . the vital point is the degree of interdependence, or, as it is commonly called, the amount of correlation." It is certain that Gall would have accepted this evaluation. Yet it is unclear, in light of the considerations just rehearsed, that a horizontal faculty psychology actually would have to predict the sorts of correlations that Gall and Spearman suppose it would; or that the failure to find such correlations would prove very much one way or the other.

The argument we've just been discussing turns on the claim that the various employments of presumptive horizontal faculties do not correlate *across cognitive domains*. But Gall has a (slightly irritating) tendency to run that argument together with one which emphasizes the failure of mental capacities to correlate *across individuals*. We'll have a quick look at this.

Every faculty psychologist has to find some motivated way of answering the question "How many faculties are there?" One way that Gall seeks to do so is to find the parameters that a psychology of individual differences would need to acknowledge, and then to postulate a distinct faculty corresponding to each such parameter. It is thus among Gall's pet arguments for distinguishing between a pair of faculties that people can differ in the degree to which they have them. Jones is good at mathematics and awful at metaphysics, and Smith has the reverse aptitudes. So the mathematical and metaphysical competences must be subserved by distinct psychological and neural mechanisms; they must be, in effect, distinct (vertical) faculties.

Now this determination to connect issues about faculties with issues about individual differences is itself something of a departure, on Gall's part, from the beaten paths of the faculty psychology tradition. As Spearman remarks:

> Through the earlier part of . . . [the] . . . historical development of the doctrine of faculties, few if any writers were much concerned with the problem . . . of the differences between individuals. The purposes for which faculties were first devised, and for a long time almost exclusively employed, had not been to portray the aspects in which men differ, but those which characterize them all alike . . . [1927, p. 29]

Nor is it entirely clear what, on Gall's view, reflection upon the existence of individual differences is supposed to add to the arguments against horizontal faculties that we reviewed just above.

The mere fact that Smith and Jones differ in their musical abilities wouldn't seem, in and of itself, to suggest the existence of a specifically musical faculty. Assume that all faculties are in fact horizontal, but that some 'mix' of such horizontal faculties is optimal for musical accomplishment (lots of perceptual acuity, say, a dash of sensibility, and very long fingers; [actually, I don't know much about music, though I do know what I like]). Well, for any such optimal mix of horizontal faculties there will surely be differences in the degree to which people approximate possessing it. If Jones outwhistles Smith, that is because his mix comes closer to the optimum than Smith's does; or so, at least, the proponent of horizontal faculties has every right to suggest, for all the argument to the contrary that we've got so far.

Perhaps, however, what Gall has in mind is this: if Smith and Jones differ in refinement of musical judgment but not, say, in refinement of practical judgment, then it must be true either of Smith or of Jones (or of both) that his musical and practical judgments are unequally refined. But if someone's musical and practical judgments can be unequally refined (or, indeed, unequally F for any F whatever), then the two kinds of judgment must ipso facto be distinct. If this *is* what is going on, however, then the individual differences argument reduces to the Leibniz' Law argument previously disapproved of.

Gall's fascination with, and insistence upon, degrees of individual difference is a most striking feature of his writings. Yet it sits badly with another of Gall's favorite themes: the repeated analogizing of faculties to instincts. That Gall apparently didn't feel the tension between these views was perhaps due to a confusion of (to put it very roughly) issues about genetic determination with issues about *species specificity*, the source of the mix-up being that certain sorts of individual differences are inherited just as species-specific psychological traits like instincts are. It may be, for example, that the ability to play really first-class baseball rests on a characteristic bundle of physiological and perceptual-motor endowments. In which case, one wouldn't be absolutely stunned to discover that that ability is inherited to some interesting extent. But of course that would be no reason to suppose that baseball is a species-specific behavior in anything like the ethologist's sense of that notion. In particular, you wouldn't want to infer from its (putative) heritability that baseball playing has a specific neurological basis, or a specific evolutionary history, or that there are genes for playing baseball. Aptitude for baseball playing, even if inherited, is patently not interestingly like an instinct.[7]

To put it in a nutshell, what is instinctive is genetically determined, but the reverse clearly doesn't have to hold. In fact, if what you have in mind by a vertical faculty is something like what the ethologist has in mind by an instinct, you probably will *not* want to postulate vertical faculties corresponding to parameters of individual differences; not even where such differences are inherited. On the contrary, in the study of instincts, the natural theoretical idealization is to a genetically and neurologically homogeneous population; instincts are forms of *species*-specific behavior. If one takes the analogy between instincts and 'fundamental powers' seriously, one must suppose—precisely contrary to the methodology that Gall endorses—that vertical faculties are to be inferred from the discovery of competences that are relatively *in*variant across subject populations.

The moral of all this critical discussion may be only that Gall's theories are sometimes more interesting than his polemics; a situation not without precedent in the history of important scientific innovations. On the other hand, if, as I believe, Gall's arguments against horizontal faculties are less persuasive than his arguments in favor of vertical ones, then the possibility remains open of a 'mixed' model in faculty psychology—one in which some but not all of the mental architecture is vertically arranged. We'll return to this later.

For now, let's put the 'problem of correlation' and the stuff about individual differences to one side. We can then distinguish four major ingredients of Gall's notion of a fundamental power: vertical faculties are *domain specific*, they are *genetically determined*, they are associated with *distinct neural structures*, and—to introduce a new point—they are *computationally autonomous*. The relevant consideration about computational autonomy is that Gall's fundamental powers do not share—and hence do not compete for—such horizontal resources as memory, attention, intelligence, judgment or whatever. This view of vertical faculties as not merely distinct in the functions they perform, but also relatively independent in the performance of their functions, will be important later when we turn to consider the notion of a cognitive module.

Suffice it, for present purposes, to note that his emphasis upon the computational autonomy of vertical faculties is one of the chief points that distinguishes Gall's theorizing from Chomsky's. For example, Chomsky (1980) suggests that there is perhaps a mathematical faculty. But, as one might expect in the light of the discussion in Part I.1, what he appears to mean by this is only part of what Gall would have meant. Chomsky's claim is primarily that some mathematical information (specifically, the idea that you can generate the natural numbers by adding one indefinitely) is innately specified. Gall would quite probably have liked that, but he would have claimed considerably more. *Qua architectural* nativist, Gall's view would be that the psychological *mechanisms* of memory, judgment, imagination, will, or whatever that mediate mathematical reasoning are themselves innately specified. *Qua vertical faculty theorist*, Gall's view would be that these mechanisms, insofar as they come into play when you do mathematics, are only nominally related to the memory, judgment, imagination . . . etc. that are engaged when you talk or commit homocides.[8] And, *qua autonomy theorist*, Gall's view would be that the mental operations that go on when you do mathematics do not much interact with and, specifically, do not much interfere with others of one's mental capacities. That we can, most of us, count and chew gum at the same time would have struck Gall as a fact that offers significant perspectives upon our mental organization.

It is important to emphasize that innateness and computational autonomy, in particular, are quite *different* properties of cognitive systems, only the first being at play in Chomsky's notion of a mental organ. Suppose, to take an extreme case, that knowledge of Peano's axioms is innate; they are not learned but genetically transmitted. It wouldn't follow, even from this radical thesis, that there is an arithmetic faculty in Gall's sense. For, the hypothesis that arithmetic knowledge is genetically transmitted is—but the vertical faculty thesis for arithmetic is not—compatible with the possibility that the psychological mechanisms that mediate arithmetic reasoning are the same ones that underlie the capacity for abstract thought in general. It is thus compatible with Chomsky's notion of a mental organ, but not with Gall's notion of a vertical faculty, that arithmetic reasoning shares (horizontal) psychological resources with jurisprudential reasoning, aesthetic reasoning, or filling out one's income tax.[9]

It is worth adding that, just as the innateness thesis for fundamental powers does not imply their organization into computationally autonomous vertical faculties, so the horizontal analysis of a cognitive capacity would not imply that that capacity is learned. Most faculty psychologists have, in point of historical fact, been nativists of the horizontal persuasion. It may be that there is use for the notion of horizontal cognitive organization, particularly in light of the possibility of a mixed model which includes both vertical and horizontal elements. It would not follow that there is much use for (or much sense to be made of) the notion that mental structures are learned. (See Fodor, 1975.) It is thus important to disentagle the horizontal faculty story from any form of Empiricism.

A final word about Gall. It seems to me that the notion of a vertical faculty is among the great historical contributions to the development of theoretical psychology. So, why isn't Gall honored in the textbooks? The story of Gall's posthumous reputation is a sad illustration of the maxim that the good men do is oft interred with their doctoral dissertations. Gall made two big mistakes, and they finished him: he believed that the degree of development of a mental organ can be measured by the relative size of the corresponding brain area, and he believed that the skull fits the brain "as a glove fits a hand." Phrenology followed as the night the day,[10] and with it all sorts of fraud and quackery, for none of which Gall was responsible but for much of which he appears to have been retrospectively blamed. It is lucky for us that we don't make mistakes any longer; those who do so clearly have little to expect from history or from the intellectual charity of their professional colleagues.

I.4. Associationism (and: 'Whatever Became of Faculty Psychology?')

I now want to take a brief look at yet a fourth way of answering the question: "How are cognitive capacities organized?" I shall refer to this tradition as 'associationism' (though I do so with some trepidation, contemporary versions of the doctrine having shed much of what the label once implied). Roughly, associationism is related to the claim that there are faculties in something like the way that phenomenalism is related to the claim that there are tables and chairs; you can take them to be incompatible, or you can read associationism as saying that faculties exist but that they have the status of constructs out of some more fundamental sort of entity. On either interpretation, however, associationists denied much of what faculty psychologists wished to assert, so that the ascendence of the former doctrine implied the decline of the latter.

Baldwin's (1911) *Dictionary of Philosophy and Psychology*—in 3 volumes, so by no means an insubstantial tome—allows "faculty psychology" a single scanty paragraph. It deserves quotation, since it illuminates the nominal (though not, I believe, the real) cause of the eclipse of that tradition.

> To say that an individual mind possesses a certain faculty is merely to say that it is capable of certain states or processes. But we find in many of the earlier psychologists a tendency to treat faculties as if they were causes, or real conditions, of

the states of processes in which they are manifested, and to speak of them as positive agencies interacting with each other. Thus persistence in voluntary decision is said to be due to extraordinary strength of will, or to will-power or to the faculty of will. Certain mental processes in man are said to have their source in the faculty of reason, and certain other processes in lower animals are explained by the existence of a faculty of instinct. This mode of pretended explanation has received the name of Faculty Psychology. Locke, in criticizing the phrase 'freedom of the will', has brought out very clearly the nature of the fallacy involved. 'We may as properly say that the singing faculty sings, and the dancing faculty dances, as that the will chooses, or that the understanding conceives. . . .'

This passage contains, by my count, one importantly false statement and two bad arguments. To begin with: it is simply not the case that "to say that an individual mind possesses a certain faculty is merely to say that it is capable of certain states or processes." There are, of necessity, far more mental capacities than there are psychological faculties on even the most inflationary census of the latter. For example, our mental capacities include the ability to add 1 plus 1, the ability to add 1 plus 2, the ability to add 1 plus 3 . . . and so on for indefinitely many drearily similar cases. And all these capacities are (presumably) to be attributed to the operation of *one and the same mathematical faculty*. The situation would not be different in any principled way if we were to assume that there is a subfaculty of the faculty of mathematics specially in charge of the addition of finite integers. You still get indefinitely much mental capacity out of each faculty you posit, this being simply a special case of the general principle that every causal agent has indefinitely many potential effects. A census of faculties is *not*, in short, equivalent to an enumeration of the capacities of the mind. What it is instead is a theory of the *structure of the causal mechanisms that underlie the mind's capacities*. It is thus perfectly possible for all hands to be agreed about what *capacities* a mind has and still to disagree about what *faculties* comprise it. Contemporary examples of such disagreements include: whether human maternal behaviors are instinctive; whether the ability to talk is an expression of 'general intelligence', etc.

Of the two bad arguments Baldwin endorses, the second—Locke's—is simply beside the point. No faculty psychologist is in fact required to say that the singing faculty sings, or that the dancing faculty dances, or that the will chooses or any such thing. He can—and should—rather say that the *organism* sings, dances, chooses, or whatever in virtue of the operation of the various faculties that it possesses. As for the understanding, it conceives one's argument only as one's stomach digests one's dinners—viz., synecdochically.

The more important of Baldwin's arguments—at least in terms of historical influence—is the first, which consists simply of a charge of vacuous hypostatization. This claim—that the postulation of mental faculties is ipso facto a form of pseudo-explanation—is practically universal in the secondary sources, the decline of the faculty tradition being attributed to widespread recognition that such postulations are indeed empty. For example, D. B. Kline (1970, p. 374) has this to say: "Subsequent criticism of (Christian Wolfe's) faculty doctrine was an elaboration of the kind of objection raised by Descartes and Locke . . . the objection revealed an appeal to faculties to be a question-begging kind of explanation as revealed by invoking an aquatic faculty to explain swimming or a terpsichorean faculty to explain dancing. This is the equivalent of substituting an impressive label for a genuine explanation, as in saying that some salve will heal a rash because it contains a therapeutic ingredient."

Connoisseurs of heavy irony will find much to please them here; for, after all, what this supposedly conclusive objection has against faculty psychology is only that faculties are individuated by their effects—i.e., that they are *functionally* individuated. And it is, of course, this very strategy of functional analysis which, according to the now standard philosophy of psychology, allows the individuation of mental constructs to steer a proper course between the unacceptable ontological alternatives of eliminative materialism on the one hand and dualism on the other. As Ned Block summarizes the doctrine in his excellent introduction to the contemporary functionalist literature (Block, 1980, p. 172): "Functionalists can be physicalists in allowing that all the entities (things, states, events, and so on) that exist are physical entities, denying only that what binds certain types of things together is a physical property. . . . Metaphysical functionalists characterize mental states in terms of their causal roles." Not to put too fine a point on it: the functionalist idea is that pain is whatever is the normal cause of pain behavior; and, mutatis mutandis, the language faculty is whatever is the normal cause of one's ability to speak. Functionalists take this line in full awareness of what Molière said about dormative virtues; and, in my view, they are quite right to do so. (For further discussion see Fodor, 1965, and 1981b.)

This is not, of course, to say that the tactic of individuating mental entities functionally is ipso facto proof against vacuous explanation. It would be a bad idea (not to say an incoherent one—see above) to postulate a faculty corresponding to each prima facie distinct behavorial capacity and let it go at that. For one thing, not all prima facie distinct behavorial capacities really do differ in their etiology, and theory construction ought to find the causal uniformities beneath the heterogeneity of surface appearances. Moreover, some capacities surely arise from the *interaction* of underlying causes; in fact, the more of these, the merrier the theorist, since his goal is to get the maximum amount of psychological explanation out of the smallest possible inventory of postulated causal mechanisms. None of this, however, has anything to do with faculty theorizing per se, since the corresponding remarks apply equally to *all* theoretical enterprises where the postulation of unobservables is at issue. Nor is it true, in point of historical fact, that faculty psychologists were particularly disposed to flout these general methodological canons. On the contrary, as Spearman (1930) correctly points out: "The general intention (in faculty theories) . . . is to represent the countless transient mental experiences by a small number of relatively permanent—particularly innate—different principles. The multitudinous actual events are thus governed by very few 'potential' ones. [Vol. 1, p. 108]. . . The theory of faculties consists essentially in deriving multitudinous processes from a few powers" (p. 155). It's hard to imagine what alternative strategy could rationally be commended.

In retrospect, then, the supposedly decisive methodological arguments against faculty theory were, on the face of them, so silly that it's hard to believe (much) in their historical significance. And, indeed, isolated arguments—like isolated experiments—generally don't alter the course of science. What usually does the job is the emergence of an alternative theoretical enterprise. As I indicated above, it seems pretty clear that what did for faculty psychology was the promise of an associationistic theory of mind. For just as Empiricist epistemology offered an account of the origin of mental *contents* which dispensed with the Cartesian postulation of innate ideas, so associationism offered an account of the ontogeny of mental *processes* which dispensed with the postulation of innate cognitive architecture—which, in short, dispensed with the need for faculties.

I take it that what an associationist (of either the classical mentalist or the more recent learning-theoretic variety) is prepared to acknowledge by way of explanatory apparatus in cognitive theory is this:

(a) A set of elements out of which psychological structures are constructed. Reflexes are the preferred elements for associationists who take it that psychological structures are behavorial; "Ideas" are the preferred elements for associationists who take it that psychological structures are mental.

(b) A relation of association defined, in the first instance, over the elements. (Only "in the first instance" because the property of being associable is preserved under association; the associative laws can apply to Ideas/Reflexes that are themselves products of association, thereby generating a distinction between elementary psychological structures and complex ones.)

(c) The laws of association. These are principles in virtue of which the character of an organism's experience determines which of its Ideas become associated or (mutatis mutandis) which conditioned reflexes get formed.

(d) Theoretically relevant parameters of the psychological structures and of the associative relations among them; so that, for example, associative relations can differ in respect of their strength and reflexes can differ in respect of their operant level.

Some associationists have been willing to acknowledge a scattering of irreducible horizontal faculties as well: for example, sensibility in the case of all the Classical Empiricists and imagination and reflection in the case of Hume and Locke respectively. But it seems clear that such concessions—often enough equivocal anyhow (see above, note 2)—are best viewed as unwilling. Ideally, according to the main stream of the associative tradition, all cognitive phenomena are to be accommodated by appeal to the very exiguous theoretical apparatus just described. As Hume says (*Enquiries*, p. 321), association is a form of attraction which "in the mental world will be found to have as extraordinary effects as (gravitational attraction does) in the natural, and to show itself in as many and as various forms."

In consequence, a profoundly reductionistic impulse has characterized much of the boldest psychological speculation in the Anglo-American tradition. The trick, for an associationist, is to show that there is nothing that faculties are required to explain, all bona fide psychological phenomena being reducible to the objects and relations enumerated in a–d. As usual, the treatment of memory provides revealing examples. So, Hume proposes to distinguish what is actually remembered from what is merely imagined not on logical grounds (you can imagine, but not remember, what didn't in fact occur), nor in terms of hypothesized differences in the underlying causal mechanisms (as a horizontal faculty psychologist would surely do) but rather by reference to the "force and vivacity" of the Ideas being entertained; whatever is remembered is assumed ipso facto to be more forceful and vivacious than anything that is merely conjured up. (Hume explains, with vast implausibility, that this is why history is always more gripping than fiction.) Hume's treatment is surely not attractive, but it exhibits in perfect microcosm the strategy of dissolving presumptive psychological mechanisms into parameters of the association relation or properties of the associated relata.

Curiously, the pursuit of this strategy sometimes led associationists to say things that sound very like Gall, though of course for quite different reasons. Thus Thorndike (of all people) echoes Gall's doctrine that there is no such thing as memory, and he cites Gall's evidence: the variability of recall across cognitive domains. Thorndike's account of this interaction is not, however, that retentiveness is a parameter of the operation of vertical faculties, but rather that it is a parameter of the association relation. "There is no memory to hold in a uniformly tight and loose grip the experiences of the past. There are only the particular connections between particular mental events and others"—which connections can vary in strength from one case to the next. (Quoted by Kline, 1970, p. 662.)

It is, of course, no accident that associationists devoted so much time to showing that the phenomena which faculties had previously been invoked to handle could be adequately explained with more parsimonious theoretical apparatus. Associationism developed in conscious and often explicit opposition to the older faculty tradition, and it was precisely the parsimony of the associationist's theory that was supposed to convince one of its scientific good repute. No Gothic proliferation of mental structures was now to be tolerated. The "how many faculties?" question would receive a *principled* answer at the associationist's hands: If a faculty is a primitive psychological mechanism—a *fundamental* power—then the answer is: "only one; only the capacity to form associations."[11]

Thus far I've been reading the associationist tradition in a way that the associationists would themselves surely have found congenial: as proposing an *alternative* to faculty psychology, one characterized by a notable reduction in the amount of theoretical apparatus to be deployed in the explanation of cognitive phenomena. In recent decades, however, a sort of revisionist reading has developed, in which associationism is viewed less as *replacing* than as *reconstructing* the theoretical mechanisms that faculty psychologists worked with. A little background discussion is required in order to see how this could be so.

As I remarked above, contemporary cognitive theory takes it for granted that the paradigmatic psychological process is a sequence of transformations of mental representations and that the paradigmatic cognitive system is one which effects such transformations. I thus assume, for purposes of this essay, that if faculties *cum* psychological mechanisms are to be acknowledged in our cognitive science, they will be computational systems of one sort or another. Now, it is a major achievement of modern logic to have shown that computational processes of any complexity whatever are reducible to (or, looked at the other way, constructible form) concatenations of surprisingly small collections of basic operations. There are a number of notations in which such constructions can be expressed, Turing machine theory and production systems being among the most familiar. Very roughly, what they have in common is the postulation of a census of computational elements on the one hand, and of combinatorial operations on the other, the output of the theory being generated by the arbitrarily iterated application of the latter to the former.

If you don't mind a little anachronism, it is not impossible to see in this sort of logical apparatus the basis for a refined and purified associationism, the idea of sets of elements with combinatorial operations specified over them being what provides the common ground. Since the logical formalism permits the construction of computational systems of arbitrary complexity, the postulation of even an elaborate population of faculties is tolerable to this new sort of associationism. For, so long as the operation of the faculties is assumed to be exhaustively computational, they can be viewed as mere constructions out of whatever elementary 'associations' the theorist is prepared to acknowledge. Perception, memory, thought, and the rest of the faculty psychologist's brood can then be accepted as distinguishable aspects of mind (specifically, as distinct mental processes) without abandoning the basic associationistic premise that practically all of the mental life is "assembled"—i.e., put together from some relatively simple and uniform population of psychological elements.

There is quite a lot of recent psychological literature which, more or less explicitly, recommends this sort of computational reinterpretation of the associative tradition. A passage from Allport (1980) will serve to give the feel of the thing:

> In the old psychology . . . linkages between a calling cue and a particular category of action were called 'habits'. The key idea . . . was that actions ('responses') are addressed or evoked by particular calling conditions ('stimuli'). If we undo the restriction that these a-b pairs must be directly observable events, and instead interpret the a's and b's as specific 'states of mind', providing in addition some relatively simple mechanisms for their interaction, then this simple associationistic conception can have surprising power. Its simplest and most direct application in information processing terms can be seen in so-called 'Production Systems'.

Allport is by no means alone in commending this line of thought. To consider just one famous example, Miller, Galanter, and Pribram in their enormously influential *Plans and the Structure of Behavior* (1960) are explicit in offering the "TOTE unit" to *replace* the reflex as the element from which complex psychological structures are to be constructed, the constructivist program itself being accepted quite without visible hesitation (or argument).

However, this marriage of concepts from associationism with concepts from computer mathematics gives evidence of being a shotgun arrangement: it's hard to recognize either the theoretical commitments of associationism or the considerations which made those commitments seem plausible, given the computational reinterpretation.

For one thing, in the traditional literature, association was viewed as a mechanical relation *among* mental contents, not as a computational relation defined over them. Hume speaks of associations between Ideas on the model of gravitational attraction between physical objects; Skinner speaks of stimuli as *eliciting* the responses conditioned to them. Now, it is important to understand that this tradition of push-pull talk in associationism is not mere unreflective metaphor. On the contrary, it is part and parcel of the associationist's rejection of mental architecture—of psychological mechanisms whose function it is to 'process' mental contents. Right at the heart of associationism is the idea that you can dispense with such mechanisms in favor of intrinsic, dynamic relations (attraction, repulsion, assimilation, and so forth) among the psychological elements themselves. This is, in its way, a brilliant—if doomed—idea (influenced, beyond any doubt, by the successes of Newtonian dynamics in physics); but it makes associationism a doctrine that is profoundly different in spirit from the picture of the mind that computational psychologists endorse.

For example, if we are to think of associated mental representations as somehow connected by *rule* rather than by mutual attraction, then we will need mechanisms to apply the rules and also places to keep them when they are not in use. (Cf. Allport: "some relatively simple mechanisms for their interaction"; no bigger than a man's hand, as one might say.) Even Turing machines exhibit a minimal architecture of tape, executive, and reader; and any remotely plausible candidate for a computational model of cognitive processes would presumably require access to considerably more such apparatus than Turing machines make do with. But this *'functional* architecture' (as it's sometimes called; see Pylyshyn, 1980) is precisely the sort of *un*reduced mental structure that real associationists wanted very much to do without. The moral is: give up the idea of dynamic relations among psychological elements in favor of the computational picture and you thereby give up a lot of what distinguishes Hume's picture of the mind from, say, Kant's.

Qualms about computational associationism are, however, by no means restricted to suspicions of historical unauthenticity. Deeper issues emerge if we ask why one should *want* to treat faculties as 'assembled' out of elementary psychological objects, even assuming the logical apparatus for effecting the construction to be available.

One answer that, of course, *won't* do is that you somehow increase the available computational power by treating faculties as constructs. On the contrary; it is a point of definition that you can't tell from the input-output capacities of a cognitive system whether it is, as it were, a primitive piece of mental architecture or something that has been put together from smaller bits. Computationally equivalent (that is, input-output equivalent) systems can, in principle, be built either way; from the point of view of an external device which communicates with them, all such systems count as the same machine. (You may be able to tell them apart because one rattles when you shake it and the other doesn't; but if so, the rattle doesn't count as part of the output.)

Moreover, similarity relations among cognitive systems far stronger than mere input/output equivalence can, in principle, be defined without broaching the issue of whether the systems should be viewed as assembled. Computer theorists, when they want to talk about computational systems in a way that abstracts from the difference between assembled and primitive processors, often speak of identities of *virtual* architecture. Roughly, you establish the virtual architecture of a machine by specifying which sets of instructions can constitute its programs. So, for example, there could be two devices, both of which can be programmed to perform simple arithmetic calculations, which are identical in *virtual* architecture in that both can execute instructions of the form 'add m to n'. However, it might be that the relation of the virtual architecture of these machines to their more elementary computational organization— and, eventually, to their physical organization—is quite different: for one of them, adding integers is a simple, primitive operation (performed, perhaps by making some measurement on voltages in a circuit); whereas, for the other, addition requires a sequence of mediating computations (as it would if the operations of a pocket calculator were to be simulated by a Turing machine). For the second machine, then, addition is an assembled operation (and, in consequence, commands to add integers must be "compiled" into the appropriate sequences of elementary operation before they can be executed). The machines may nevertheless be identical (not only in their input/output functions but also) in the set of programs they can run; hence the possibility of identical virtual architecture between machines that are 'hardwired' in the one case and assembled in the other. In approximately this way, a traditional faculty psychologist and an associationist might end up agreeing about the virtual architecture of cognitive capacities, but disagreeing about whether the psychological mechanisms which mediate these capacities ought to be viewed as constructs.

Well, to end this excursis, the present question is why anything except virtual architecture should be of any interest to the psychologist; why, in particular, should anybody *care* whether faculties are assembled? What I think many cognitive scientists find persuasive—not to say mandatory—about the constructivist alternative is certain ontogenetic possibilities that it appears to offer. Specifically, if mental structures can be viewed as assembled from primitive elements, then perhaps mechanisms of *learning* can be shown to be responsible for effecting their construction. Here, then, is a real convergence between the motivations of classical associationism and those which actuate its computational reincarnation: Both doctrines find in constructivist analyses of mental structures the promise of an Empiricist (i.e., non-Nativist) theory of cognitive development.

But not, I think, with equal plausibility. We have seen that computational associationists are free to dispense with previously accepted constraints upon the sorts of mental structures that associationism can acknowledge; in principle, any computational mechanism can be reconstructed with the apparatus they have available. Arguably, however, it was only in light of his insistence upon an absolute *minimum* of virtual architecture that the classical associationist's Empiricism was remotely plausible.

The basic point about association was, surely, that it offered a mechanism for bringing about co-occurrence relations among *mental* events which mirror the corresponding relations among *environmental* ones. The feature of experience to which the formation of associations was supposed to be most sensitive was thus relative frequencies of spatiotemporal contiguities among stimuli (Ideas become associated in virtue of spatiotemporal propinquities among the things that they are Ideas *of*; responses get conditioned in virtue of spatiotemporal propinquities between discriminative and reinforcing stimuli; and so forth). Correspondingly, the typical products of association are chains of Ideas (mutatis mutandis, response chains), these being the psychological counterparts of causal chains of environmental events. Not to put too fine a point on it, association was a mechanism for producing sequential redundancies in the mind (or in behavior) which mirror sequential redundancies in the world. This notion of mental structures, and of the environmental structures presumed to cause them, is no doubt depressingly crude; but at least one can imagine such associative chains being constructed from their elementary links under the influence of environmental regularities of the sorts that organisms actually do encounter. To that extent the classical associationist's ontogenetic theories fit together with his account of the structure of mature cognitive competence.

What the computational associationist offers instead is the possibility of mental structures of arbitrary complexity; he thus has a sort of guaranty that his associationism will never force him to accept an unduly impoverished notion of mental organization. But he pays a price: traditional associationist accounts of ontogeny can no longer be relied upon. There is simply no reason at all to believe that the ontogeny of the elaborate psychological organization that computational associationism contemplates can be explained by appeal to learning principles which do what principles of associative learning did—viz., create mental copies of environmental redundancies. In particular, the constructibility *in logical principle* of arbitrarily complicated processes from elementary ones doesn't *begin* to imply that such processes are constructible *in ontogeny* by the operation of any learning mechanism of a kind that associationists would be prepared to live with. This is a point about which I suspect that many contemporary psychologists are profoundly confused.

In short, as the operative notion of mental structure gets richer, it becomes increasingly difficult to imagine identifying the ontogeny of such structures with the registration of environmental regularities. Hence the main course of recent Cartesian theorizing, with its reiterated emphasis upon 'poverty of the stimulus' arguments: There would seem not to be enough ambient information available to account for the functional architecture that minds are found to have. You can, no doubt, make a language parser, or a visual scene recognizer, or a 'General Problem Solver' out of the sort of psychological elements that computational associationists acknowledge; this follows just from the assumption that parsers and scene recognizers and the rest are species of computers. What does *not* follow is that there is some way of constructing such systems from the information given *in experience*. But this consideration undermines the main motivation for viewing mental structures as assembled in the first place—viz., that what is first exhibited as *assembled* can then be exhibited as *learned*—indeed, as learned *by association*. To put the point in a nutshell, the crucial difference between classical and computational associationism is simply that the latter is utterly lacking in any theory of learning. (There is, once again, a budget of heavy ironies to contemplate. After all, the historical point of associationism was largely to make Empiricism respectable. It was to do this precisely by providing a theory of learning which would show how mental structure could be accounted for without nativistic postulation. There was a guy in Greek mythology who got so hungry that eventually he ate himself; modern associationism may be said to have attained much the same condition.)

My present purposes being largely expository, I don't propose to pursue this line of argument; it is, in any event, familiar from Chomsky's work. Suffice it that insofar as environmentalist biases provide a main motivation for the computational associationist's constructivism, it is perhaps best seen as a failed attempt at reconciling faculty psychology with Empiricism. Conversely, latter-day nativists typically view constructivism in psychology with deep misgivings; if mental architecture is innately specified and if the ontogeny of cognition is primarily the unfolding of a genetic program, why should one expect that mental structures will prove to be assembled? The idea that they are hardwired—i.e., that the grain of their physical architecture quite closely parallels the grain of their virtual architecture—seems at least equally plausible.

As the last paragraph should suggest, neurological speculations are quite close to the surface here. Perhaps you can't tell from *outside* whether a computational system is assembled or primitive, but you certainly ought to be able to tell from *inside*. The view of faculties as assembled comports with a view of the corresponding neurology as, at least initially, diffuse and equipotential; environmental tuition may effect local alterations in connectivity (for example), but it would be astonishing if it produced neural architecture and neural specificity on a large scale. By contrast, since the traditional faculty psychologist is a nativist down to his boots, he predicts a brain that is parsed into big, perhaps even macroscopic, neural structures. In this respect at least, the tradition that includes Gall runs through Wernicke and Broca (see Caplan, 1981).

This is, no doubt, all pretty loose—a matter less of demonstrative arguments than of elective affinities. Thus the constructivist may be interested in formalisms with the expressive power of universal computers, but I doubt that anybody actually thinks that the brain is really much like a Turing machine. Nor does the adjudication between virtual architecture and physical structure have to be made in the same way for every faculty; it is perfectly possible that operations that are primitive in one cognitive process may be assembled in another. For that matter, innately specified computational systems *could*, in logical principle, be put together from elementary operations; and learning *could*, in logical principle, result in elaborate and specific neural morphology. All we have is that neither of these contingencies seems very likely as a matter of fact. Let's leave it at this: the standard reason for stressing the distinction between virtual and physical architecture is to exhibit the actual organization of the mind as just one of the possibilities that could have been realized had the environment dictated an alternative arrangement of the computational elements. And a natural interpretation of neural hardwiring is that it packages into unanalyzed operations what may be quite powerful primitive computational capacities.

This looks like a good place for a little summary and prospectus.

Summary: In effect, what we have done so far is to suggest a number of questions that one can ask about a cognitive system in aid of locating it in relation to a general taxonomy of such systems. In particular:

1. Is it domain specific, or do its operations cross content domains? This is, of course, the question of vertical versus horizontal cognitive organization; Gall versus Plato.

2. Is the computational system innately specified, or is its structure formed by some sort of learning process?

3. Is the computational system 'assembled' (in the sense of having been put together from some stock of more elementary subprocesses) or does its virtual architecture map relatively directly onto its neural implementation?

4. Is it hardwired (in the sense of being associated with specific, localized, and elaborately structured neural systems) or is it implement by relatively equipotential neural mechanisms?

5. Is it computationally autonomous (in Gall's sense), or does it share horizontal resources (of memory, attention, or whatever) with other cognitive systems?

Prospectus: I now propose to use this taxonomic apparatus to introduce the notion of a *cognitive module*. Two preliminary points, however. First, each of questions 1–5 is susceptible to a 'more or less' sort of answer. One would thus expect—what anyhow seems to be desirable—that the notion of modularity ought to admit of degrees. The notion of modularity that I have in mind certainly does. When I speak of a cognitive system as modular, I shall therefore always mean "to some interesting extent." Second, I am not, in any strict sense, in the business of 'defining my terms'. I don't think that theoretical terms usually have definitions (for that matter, I don't think that nontheoretical terms usually do either). And, anyhow, the taxonomic apparatus just sketched is incomplete; what I take to be perhaps the most important aspect of modularity— something that I shall call "informational encapsulation"—has yet to appear. So what I propose to do instead of defining "modular" is to associate the notion with a pattern of answers to such questions as 1–5. Roughly, modular cognitive systems are domain specific, innately specified, hardwired, autonomous, and not assembled. Since modular systems are domain-specific computational mechanisms, it follows that they are species of vertical faculties.

I shall assume, hopefully, that this gives us a notion of modularity that is good enough to work with. The rest of this essay is devoted to doing the work. First, I want to try to refine the modularity concept by enriching the taxonomy. The goal is to suggest more properties that modular systems might have in common than the ones just mentioned, and also to try to see what it is that underlies the taxonomy: Why should there be modular systems? Why does this cluster of properties tend to co-occur? Second, I want to say something about the extension of the concept; to propose a hypothesis about which cognitive systems are, in fact, modular. This second line of inquiry will provide the main structure of the discussion, the first emerging as opportunity provides targets. By the time I've finished, I shall have made the following suggestions:

(a) That the set of processors for which the modularity view currently seems most convincing is coextensive with a functionally definable subset of the cognitive systems.

(b) That there is some (more or less a priori) reason to believe that cognitive systems which do *not* belong to that functionally defined subset may be, in important respects, *non*modular (e.g., mediated by horizontal faculties). And finally,

(c) I shall make some depressed remarks along the following lines: though the putatively nonmodular processes include some of the ones that we would most like to know about (thought, for example, and the fixation of belief), our cognitive science has in fact made approximately no progress in studying these processes, and this may well be *because* of their nonmodularity. It may be that, from the point of view of practicable research strategy, it is only the modular cognitive systems that we have any serious hope of understanding. In which case, convincing arguments for nonmodularity should be received with considerable gloom.

PART II
A FUNCTIONAL TAXONOMY OF COGNITIVE MECHANISMS

I want to argue that the current best candidates for treatment as *modular* cognitive systems share a certain functional role in the mental life of organisms; the discussion in this section is largely devoted to saying which functional role that is. As often happens in playing cognitive science, it is helpful to characterize the functions of psychological systems by analogy to the organization of idealized computing machines. So, I commence with a brief digression in the direction of computers.

When philosophers of mind think about computers, it is often Turing machines that they are thinking about. And this is understandable. If there is an interesting analogy between minds qua minds and computers qua computers, it ought to be possible to couch it as an analogy between minds and Turing machines, since a Turing machine is, in a certain sense, as general as any kind of computer can be. More precisely: if, as many of us now suppose, minds are essentially symbol-manipulating devices, it ought to be useful to think of minds on the Turing-machine model since Turing machines are (again "in a certain sense") as general as any symbol-manipulating device can be.

However, as we have already had reason to observe, Turing machines are also very simple devices; their functional architecture is exhaustively surveyed when we have mentioned a small number of interacting subsystems (tape, scanner, printer, and executive) and a small inventory of primitive machine operations (stop, start, move the tape, read the tape, change state, print). Moreover—and this is the point of present concern—Turing machines are *closed computational systems*; the sole determinants of their computations are the current machine state, the tape configuration, and the program, the rest of the world being quite irrelevant to the character of their performance; whereas, of course, organisms are forever exchanging information with their environments, and much of their psychological structure is constituted of mechanisms which function to mediate such exchanges. If, therefore, we are to start with anything like Turing machines as models in cognitive psychology, we must think of them as embedded in a matrix of subsidiary systems which affect their computations in ways that are responsive to the flow of environmental events. The function of these subsidiary systems is to provide the central machine with information about the world; information expressed by mental symbols in whatever format cognitive processes demand of the representations that they apply to.

I pause to note that the format constraint on the subsidiary systems is vital. *Any* mechanism whose states covary with environmental ones can be thought of as registering information about the world; and, given the satisfaction of certain further conditions, the output of such systems can reasonably be thought of as *representations* of the environmental states with which they covary. (See Dretske, 1981; Stampe, 1977; Fodor, forthcoming.) But if cognitive processors are *computational* systems, they have access to such information solely in virtue of the *form* of the representations in which it is couched. Computational processes are, by definition, *syntactic*; a device which makes information available to such processes is therefore responsible for its format as well as its quality. If, for example, we think of such a device as writing on the tape of a Turing machine, then it must write *in a language that the machine can understand* (more precisely, in the language in which the machine computes). Or, to put it in a psychological-sounding way, if we think of the perceptual mechanisms as analogous to such devices, then we are saying that *what perception must do is to so represent the world as to make it accessible to thought.* The condition on appropriateness of format is by way of emphasizing that not every representation of the world will do for this purpose.

I wish that I knew what to call the "subsidiary systems" that perform this function. Here are some possibilities that I have considered and—with varying degrees of reluctance—decided to reject:

—'Perceptual systems' would be the obvious choice except that, as we shall presently see, perception is not the only psychological mechanism that functions to present the world to thought, and I would like a term broad enough to embrace them all. Moreover, as will also become apparent, there are important reasons for not viewing the subsidiary systems as effecting the fixation of belief. By contrast, perception is a mechanism of belief fixation par excellence: the normal consequence of a perceptual transaction is the acquisition of a perceptual belief. (Having entered this caveat, I shall nevertheless often speak of the subsidiary systems as mechanisms of perceptual analysis. For most purposes it is harmless to do so and it does simplify the exposition.)

—I have sometimes thought of calling these subsidiary systems 'compilers', thereby stressing that their output consists of representations that are accessible to relatively central computational processes. But that way of talking leads to difficulties too. Real compilers are functions from programs onto programs, programs themselves being (approximately) sequences of instructions. But not much of what perception makes available to thought is plausibly viewed as a program. Indeed, it is partly the attempt to force perceptual information into that mold which engenders procedural semantics, the identification of perceptual categories with action schemes, and other such aberrations of theory. (For discussion, see Fodor, 1981a, chapter 8.)

—One could try calling them 'transducers' except that, on at least one usual understanding (see Lowenstein, 1960), transducers are analog systems that take proximal stimulations onto more or less precisely covarying neural signals. Mechanisms of transduction are thus *contrasted* with computational mechanisms: whereas the latter may perform quite complicated, inference-like transformations, the former are supposed—at least ideally—to preserve the informational content of their inputs, altering *only* the format in which the information is displayed. We shall see, however, that representations at the interface between (what I have been calling) 'subsidiary' and 'central' systems exhibit levels of encoding that are quite abstractly related to the play of proximal stimulation.

Pylyshyn and I (1981) have called these subsidiary systems 'compiled transducers', using the 'compiled' part to indicate that they have an internal computational structure and the 'transducer' part to indicate that they exhibit a certain sort of informational encapsulation that will presently loom large in this discussion. I think that usage is all right given the explication, but it admittedly hasn't much to do with the conventional import of these terms and thus probably produces as much confusion as it avoids.

It is, perhaps, not surprising that computer theory provides no way of talking that does precisely the job I want to do. Computers generally interface with their environments *via some human being* (which is what makes them computers rather than robots). The programmer thus takes on the function of the subsidiary computational systems that I have been struggling to describe—viz., by providing the machine with information about the world in a form in which the machine can use it. Surprising or not, however, it is a considerable nuisance. Ingenuity having failed me completely, I propose to call them variously 'input systems', or 'input analyzers' or, sometimes, 'interface systems'. At least this terminology emphasizes that they operate relatively early on. I rely on the reader to keep it in mind, however, that input systems are *post*-transductive mechanisms according to my usage. Also that switches from one of the epithets to another usually signify no more than a yen for stylistic variation.

So, then, we are to have a trichotomous functional taxonomy of psychological processes; a taxonomy which distinguishes transducers, input systems, and central processors, with the flow of input information becoming accessible to these mechanisms in about that order. These categories are intended to be exclusive but not, of course, to exhaust the types of psychological mechanisms that a theory of cognition might have reason to postulate. Since the trichotomy is not exhaustive, it is left wide open that there may be modular systems that do not subserve any of these functions. Among the obvious candidates would be systems involved in the motor integration of such behaviors as speech and locomotion. It would please me if the kinds of arguments that I shall give for the modularity of input systems proved to have application to motor systems as well. But I don't propose to investigate that possibility here.

Input systems function to get information into the central processors; specifically, they mediate between transducer outputs and central cognitive mechanisms by encoding the mental representations which provide domains for the operations of the latter. This does not mean, however, that input systems *translate* from the representations that transducers afford into representations in the central code. On the contrary, translation preserves informational content and, as I remarked above, the computations that input systems perform typically do not. Whereas transducer outputs are most naturally interpreted as specifying the distribution of stimulations at the 'surfaces' (as it were) of the organism, the input systems deliver representations that are most naturally interpreted as characterizing the arrangement of *things in the world*. Input analyzers are thus inference-performing systems within the usual limitations of that metaphor. Specifically, the inferences at issue have as their 'premises' transduced representations of proximal stimulus configurations, and as their 'conclusions' representations of the character and distribution of distal objects.

It is hard to see how a computer could fail to exhibit mechanisms of transduction if it is to interface with the world at all. But is is perfectly possible to imagine a machine whose computations are appropriately sensitive to environmental events but which does *not* exhibit a functional distinction between input systems and central systems. Roughly, endorsing this computational architecture is tantamount to insisting upon a perception/cognition distinction. It is tantamount to claiming that a certain class of computational problems of 'object identification' (or, more correctly, a class of computational problems whose solutions consist in the recovery of certain proprietary descriptions of objects) has been 'detached' from the domain of cognition at large and handed over to functionally distinguishable psychological mechanisms. Perceptual analysis is, according to this model, not, strictly speaking, a species of thought. (The reader is again reminded, however, that the identification of input processing with perceptual analysis is itself only approximate. This will all presently sort itself out; I promise.)

Given the possibility in principle that the perceptual mechanisms could be continuous with the higher cognitive processes, one is tempted to ask what the point of a trichotomous functional architecture could be. What, teleologically speaking, might it buy for an organism that has transducers and central cognitive processors to have input analyzers as well? I think there probably *is* an answer to this question: Implicit in the trichotomous architecture is the isolation of perceptual analysis from certain effects of background belief and set; and, as we shall see, this has implications for both the speed and the objectivity of perceptual integration. It bears emphasis, however, that putting the teleological issues in the way I just did involves some fairly dubious evolutionary assumptions. To suppose that the issue is *Why, given that there are central processors, should there be input systems as well?* is to take for granted that the former should be viewed as philogenetically prior to the latter. However, an equally plausible story might have it the other way 'round—viz., that input analyzers, with their (as I shall argue) relatively rigid domain specificity and automaticity of functioning, are the aboriginal prototypes of inference-making psychological systems. Cognitive evolution would thus have been in the direction of gradually freeing certain sorts of problem-solving systems from the constraints under which input analyzers labor—hence of producing, as a relatively late achievement, the comparatively domain-free inferential capacities which apparently mediate the higher flights of cognition. (See Rozen, 1976, where the plausibility of this picture of cognitive phylogeny is impressively defended.)

In any event, the justification for postulating a functionally individuated class of input analyzers distinct from central cognitive mechanisms must finally rest on two sorts of evidence: I have to show that there are interesting things that the input analyzers have in common; and I have to show that there are interesting respects in which they differ from cognitive processes at large. The second of these burdens will be taken up in Part IV. For now, I am going to argue that the functionally specified class *input system* does pick out a "natural kind" for purposes of psychological theory construction; that there are, in fact, lots of interesting things to say about the common properties of the mechanisms that mediate input analysis.

There is, however, one more preliminary point to make before getting down to that business. To claim that the functional category *input system* picks out a natural kind is to endorse an eccentric taxonomy of cognitive processes. Eyebrows should commence to be raised starting here. For, if you ask "which *are* the psychological mechanisms that can plausibly be thought of as functioning to provide information about the distal environment in a format appropriate for central processing?" the answer would seem to be "the perceptual systems *plus language*." And this is, from the point of view of traditional ways of carving things up, an odd category.

The traditional taxonomy goes something like this: perception (vision, audition, or whatever) on the one side, and thought-and-language (the representational processes) on the other. Now, the representational character of language is self-evdient, and I don't doubt the theoretical importance of the representational character of thought. (On the contrary, I think that it is *the* essential fact that an adequate theory of the propositional attitudes would have to account for. (See Fodor, 1981a, chapter 7.)) But we're not, of course, committed to there being only one right way of assigning psychological mechanisms to functional classes. The present claim is that, for purposes of assessing the issues about modularity, a rather different taxonomy proves illuminating.

Well then, what precisely *is* the functional similarity between language mechanisms and perceptual mechanisms in virtue of which both count as 'input systems'? There is, of course, the obvious point that utterances (e.g., sentence tokens) are themselves objects to be perceptually identified, just as mountains, teacups, and four-alarm fires are. Understanding a token sentence presumably involves assigning it a structural description, this being part and parcel of computing a token-to-type relation; and that is precisely the sort of function we would expect an input system to perform. However, in stressing the functional analogy between language and perception, I have something more in mind than the fact that understanding utterances is itself a typical perceptual process.

I've said that input systems function to interpret transduced information and to make it available to central processes; and that, in the normal case, what they provide will be information about the "layout" (to borrow a term of Gibson's) of distal stimuli. How might such a system work? Heaven knows there are few harder questions; but I assume that, in the case of perception, the answer must include some such story as the following. The character of transducer outputs is determined, in some lawful way, by the character of impinging energy at the transducer surface; and the character of the energy at the transducer surface is itself lawfully determined by the character of the distal layout. Because there are regularities of this latter sort, it is possible to infer properties of the distal layout from corresponding properties of the transducer output. Input analyzers are devices which perform inferences of this sort.

A useful example is Ullman's (1979) algorithm for inferring "form from motion" in visual perception. Under assumptions (e.g., of rigidity) that distal stimuli usually satisfy, a specific sequence of transformations of the energy distributions at the retina will be reliably interpretable as having been caused by (and hence as specifying) the spatial displacement of a distal object of determinate three-dimensional shape. A device that has access to the transducer outputs can infer this shape by executing Ullman's (or some equivalent) algorithm. I assume that performing such computations is precisely the function of input systems, Ullman's case being unusual primarily in the univocality with which the premises of the perceptual inference warrant its conclusion.

Now about language: Just as patterns of visual energy arriving at the retina are correlated, in a complicated but regular way, with certain properties of distal layouts, so too are the patterns of auditory energy that excite the tympanic membrane in speech exchanges. With, of course, this vital difference: What underwrites the correlation between visual stimulations and distal layouts are (roughly) the laws of light reflectance. Whereas, what underwrites the correlation between token utterances and distal layouts is (roughly) a convention of truth-telling. In the root case, the convention is that we say of x that it is F only if x is F. Because that convention holds, it is possible to infer from what one hears said to the way that the world is.[12]

Of course, in neither the linguistic nor the perceptual case is the information so provided infallible. The world often isn't the way it looks to be or the way that people say it is. But, equally of course, input systems don't have to deliver apodictic truths in order to deliver quite useful information. And, anyhow, *the operation of the input systems should not be identified with the fixation of belief*. What we *believe* depends on the evaluation of how things look, or are said to be, *in light of background information* about (inter alia) how good the seeing is or how trustworthy the source. Fixation of belief is *just* the sort of thing I have in mind as a typical *central* process.

So much, then, for the similarity of function between the lingusitic and the perceptual systems: both serve to get information about the world into a format appropriate for access by such central processes as mediate the fixation of belief. But now, is there anything to be said for exploiting this analogy? What, from the point of view of psychological theory, do we gain by postulating a functional class of perceptual-and-linguistic processes? Clearly, the proof of this pudding is *entirely* in the eating. I'm about to argue that, if we undertake to build a psychology that acknowledges this functional class as a neutral kind, we discover that the processes we have grouped together do indeed have many interesting properties in common—properties the possession of which is not entailed by their functional homogeneity. (I take it that that is what a natural kind is: a class of phenomena that have many scientifically interesting properties in common over and above whatever properties define the class.) In the present case, what the input systems have in common besides their functional similarities can be summarized in a phrase: *input systems are modules*. A fortiori, they share those properties that are characteristic of vertical faculties. Input systems are—or so I'll argue—what Gall was right about.

What follows is the elaboration of that claim, together with an occasional glimpse at the state of the evidence. I should say at the outset that not every psychologist would agree with me about what the state of the evidence is. I am arguing well in advance of (and, in some places, a little in the face of) the currently received views. So, perhaps one should take this exercise as in part a thought experiment: I'll be trying to say what you might expect the data to look like if the modularity story is true of input systems; and I'll claim that, insofar as any facts are known, they seem to be generally compatible with such expectations.

PART III
INPUT SYSTEMS AS MODULES

The modularity of the input systems consists in their possession of most or all of the properties now to be enumerated. If there are other psychological systems which possess most or all of these properties then, of course, they are modular too. It is, however, a main thesis of this work that the properties in virtue of which input systems are modular are ones which, in general, central cognitive processes do not share.

III.1. Input systems are domain specific

Let's start with this: how many input systems are there? The discussion thus far might be construed so as to suggest an answer somewhere in the vicinity of six—viz., one for each of the traditional sensory/perceptual 'modes' (hearing, sight, touch, taste, smell) and one more for language. This is *not*, however, the intended doctrine; what is proposed is something much more in the spirit of Gall's bumps. I imagine that within (and, quite possibly, across)[13] the traditional modes, there are highly specialized computational mechanisms in the business of generating hypotheses about the distal sources of proximal stimulations. The specialization of these mechanisms consists in constraints either on the range of information they can access in the course of projecting such hypotheses, or in the range of distal properties they can project such hypotheses about, or, most usually, on both.

Candidates might include, in the case of vision, mechanisms for color perception, for the analysis of shape, and for the analysis of three-dimensional spatial relations.[14] They might also include quite narrowly task-specific 'higher level' systems concerned with the visual guidance of bodily motions or with the recognition of faces of conspecifics. Candidates in audition might include computational systems that assign grammatical descriptions to token utterances; or ones that detect the melodic or rhythmic structure of acoustic arrays; or, for that matter, ones that mediate the recognition of the *voices* of conspecifics. There is, in fact, some evidence for the domain specificity of several of the systems just enumerated, but I suggest the examples primarily by way of indicating the levels of grain at which input systems might be modularized.

What, then, are the arguments for the domain specificity of input systems? To begin with, there is a sense in which input systems are ipso facto domain specific in a way in which computational systems at large are not. This is, however, quite uninteresting, a merely semantic point. Suppose, for example, that the function of the mechanisms of visual perception is to map transduced patterns of retinal excitation onto formulas of some central computational code. Then it follows trivially that their computational domain *qua mechanisms of visual perception* is specific to the class of possible retinal outputs. Correspondingly, if what the language-processing mechanisms do is pair utterance tokens with central formulas, then their computational domains *qua mechanisms of language processing* must be whatever encodings of utterances the auditory transducers produce. In similar boring fashion, the psychological mechanisms that mediate the perception of cows are ipso facto domain specific *qua mechanisms of cow perception*.

From such truisms, it goes without saying, nothing useful follows. In particular, the modularity of a system cannot be inferred from this trivial kind of domain specificity. It is, for example, entirely compatible with the cow specificity of cow perception that the recognition of cows should be mediated by precisely the same mechanisms that effect the perception of language, or of earthquakes, or of three-masted brigantines. For example, all four could perfectly well be accomplished by one and the same set of horizontal faculties. The interesting notion of domain specificity, by contrast, is Gall's idea that there are distinct psychological mechanisms— *vertical* faculties— corresponding to distinct stimulus domains. It is this latter claim that's now at issue.

Evidence for the domain specificity of an input analyzer can be of a variety of different sorts. Just occasionally the argument is quite direct and the demonstrations correspondingly dramatic. For example, there are results owing to investigators at the Haskins Laboratories which strongly suggest the domain specificity of the perceptual systems that effect the phonetic analysis of speech. The claim is that these mechanisms are different from those which effect the perceptual analysis of auditory nonspeech, and the experiments show that how a signal sounds to the hearer does depend, in rather startling ways, on whether the acoustic context indicates that the stimulus is an utterance. Roughly, the very same signal that is heard as the onset of a consonant when the context specifies that the stimulus is speech is heard as a "whistle" or "glide" when it is isolated from the speech stream. The rather strong implication is that the computational systems that come into play in the perceptual analysis of speech are distinctive in that they operate *only* upon acoustic signals that are taken to be utterances. (See Liberman et al., 1967; for further discussion, see Fodor, Bever, and Garrett, 1974).

The Haskins experiments demonstrate the domain specificity of an input analyzer by showing that only a relatively restricted class of stimulations can throw the switch that turns it on. There are, however, other kinds of empirical arguments that can lead to the same sort of conclusions. One that has done quite a lot of work for cognitive scientists goes like this: If you have an *eccentric* stimulus domain—one in which perceptual analysis requires a body of information whose character and content is specific to that domain— then it is plausible that psychological processes defined over that domain may be carried out by relatively special purpose computational systems. All things being equal, the plausibility of this speculation is about proportional to the eccentricity of the domain.

Comparing perceiving cows with perceiving sentences will help to show what's going on here. I really have no idea how cow perception works, but let's follow the fashions and suppose, for purposes of discussion, that we use some sort of prototype-plus-similarity-metric. That is, the perceptual recognition of cows is effected by some mechanism which provides solutions for computational problems of the form: how similar—how 'close'—is the distal stimulus to a prototypical cow? My point is that *if* that's the way it's done, then cow perception might be mediated by much the same mechanisms that operate in a large variety of other perceptual domains as well—in fact, in any domain that is organized around prototypes. This is because we can imagine a quite general computational system which, given a specification of a prototype and a similarity metric for an arbitrary domain of percepts, will then compute the relevant distance relations in that domain. It seems plausible, that is to say, that procedures for estimating the distance between an input and a perceptual prototype should have pretty much the same computational structure wherever they are encountered.

It is, however, most unlikely that the perceptual recognition of sentences should be mediated by such procedures, and that is because sentence tokens constitute a set of highly eccentric stimuli: All the available evidence suggests that the computations which sentence recognizers perform must be closely tuned to a complex of stimulus properties that is quite specific to sentences. Roughly, the idea is that the structure of the sentence recognition system is responsive to universal properties of language and hence that the system works only in domains which exhibit these properties.

I take it that this story is by now pretty well known. The argument goes like this: Consider the class of *nomologically possible human languages*. There is evidence that this class constitutes quite a small subset of the logically possible linguistic systems. In particular, the nomologically possible human languages include only the ones that satisfy a set of (contingent) generalizations known as the 'linguistic universals.' One way to find out something about what linguistic universals there are is by examining and comparing *actual* human languages (French, English, Urdu, or whatever) with an eye to determining which properties they have in common. Much work in linguistics over the last twenty-five years or so has pursued this strategy, and a variety of candidate linguistic universals have been proposed, both in phonology and in syntax.

It seems quite unlikely that the existence of these universals is merely fortuitous, or that they can be explained by appeal to historical affinities among the languages that share them or by appeal to whatever pragmatic factors may operate to shape communication systems. (By pragmatic factors, I mean ones that involve general properties of communication exchanges as such, including the utilities of the partners to the exchanges. So, for example, Putnam (1961) once suggested that there are grammatical transformations because communicative efficiency is served by the deletion of redundant portions of messages, etc.) The obvious alternative to such accounts is to assume that the universals represent biases of a species-specific language-learning system, and a number of proposals have been made about how, in detail, such systems might be pretuned. It is assumed, according to all these accounts, that the language-learning mechanisms 'know about' the universals and operate only in domains in which the universals are satisfied. (For a review, see Pinker, 1979.)

Parity of argument suggests that a similar story should hold for the mechanisms of language *perception*. In particular, the perceptual system involved is presumed to have access to information about how the universals are realized in the language it applies to. The upshot of this line of thought is that the perceptual system for a language comes to be viewed as containing quite an elaborate theory of the objects in its domain; perhaps a theory couched in the form of a grammar of the language. Correspondingly, the process of perceptual recognition is viewed as the application of that theory to the analysis of current inputs. (For some recent work on the parsing of natural language, see Marcus, 1977; Kaplan and Bresnan, in press; and Frazier and Fodor, 1978. All these otherwise quite different approaches share the methodological framework just outlined.)

To come to the moral: Since the satisfaction of the universals is supposed to be a property that distinguishes sentences from other stimulus domains, the more elaborate and complex the theory of universals comes to be the more eccentric the stimulus domain for sentence recognition. And, as we remarked above, the more eccentric a stimulus domain, the more plausible the speculation that it is computed by a special-purpose mechanism. It is, in particular, very hard to see how a device which classifies stimuli in respect of distance from a prototype could be recruited for purposes of sentence recognition. The computational question in sentence recognition seems to be not "How far to the nearest prototype?" but rather "How does the theory of the language apply to the analysis of the stimulus now at hand?"

There are probably quite a lot of kinds of relatively eccentric stimulus domains—ones whose perceptual analysis requires information that is highly specific to the domain in question. The organization of sentence perception around syntactic and phonological information does not exhaust the examples even in the case of language. So, for a further example, it is often and plausibly proposed that the processes that mediate phone recognition must have access to an internal model of the physical structure of the vocal apparatus. The argument is that a variety of constancies in speech perception seem to have precisely the effect of undoing garble that its inertial properties produce when the vocal mechanism responds to the phonetic intentions of the speaker. If this hypothesis is correct, then phone recognition is quite closely tuned to the mechanisms of speech production (see note 13). Once again, highly tuned computations are suggestive of special-purpose processors. Analogous points could be made in other perceptual modes. Faces are favorite candidates for eccentric stimuli (see Yin, 1969, 1970; Carey, 1978); and as I mentioned above, Ullman's work has made it seem plausible that the visual recognition of three-dimensional form is accomplished by systems that are tuned to the eccentricities of special classes of rigid spatial transformations.

From our point of view, the crucial question in all such examples is: how good is the inference from the eccentricity of the stimulus domain to the specificity of the corresponding psychological mechanisms? I am, in fact, not boundlessly enthusiastic about such inferences; they are clearly a long way from apodictic. Chess playing, for example, exploits a vast amount of eccentric information, but nobody wants to postulate a chess faculty. (Well, *almost* nobody. It is of some interest that recent progress in the artificial intelligence of chess has been achieved largely by employing specialized hardware. And, for what it's worth, chess is notably one of those cognitive capacities which breeds prodigies; so it is a candidate for modularity by Gall's criteria if not by mine.) Suffice it, for the present to suggest that it is probably characteristic of many modular systems that they operate in eccentric domains, since a likely motive for modularizing a system is that the computations it performs are idiosyncratic. But the converse inference—from the eccentricity of the domain to the modularity of the system—is warranted by nothing stronger than the maxim: specialized systems for specialized tasks. The most transparent situation is thus the one where you have a mechanism that computes an eccentric domain and is also modular by independent criteria; the eccentricity of the domain rationalizes the modularity of the processor and the modularity of the processor goes some way towards explaining how the efficient computation of eccentric domains is possible.

III.2   *The operation of input systems is mandatory*

You can't help hearing an utterance of a sentence (in a language you know) as an utterance of a sentence, and you can't help seeing a visual array as consisting of objects distributed in three-dimensional space. Similarly, mutatis mutandis, for the other perceptual modes: you can't, for instance, help feeling what you run your fingers over as the surface of an object.[15] Marslen-Wilson and Tyler (1981), discussing word recognition, remark that ". . . even when subjects are asked to focus their attention on the acoustic-phonetic properties of the input, they do not seem to be able to avoid identifying the words involved. . . . This implies that the kind of processing operations observable in spoken-word recognition are mediated by automatic processes which are obligatorily applied . . . (p. 327).

The fact that input systems are apparently constrained to apply whenever they can apply is, when one thinks of it, rather remarkable. There is every reason to believe that, in the general case, the computational relations that input systems mediate—roughly, the relations between transducer outputs and percepts—are quite remote. For example, on all current theories, it requires elaborate processing to get you from the representation of a proximal stimulus that the retina provides to a representation of the distal stimuli as an array of objects in space.[16] Yet we apparently have no choice but to take up this computational burden whenever it is offered. In short, the operation of the input systems appears to be, in this respect, inflexibly insensitive to the character of one's utilities. You can't hear speech as noise *even if you would prefer to.*

What you can do, of course, is choose not to hear it at all—viz., not attend.[17] In the interesting cases—where this is achieved without deactivating a transducer (e.g., by sticking your fingers in your ears)—the strategy that works best is rather tortuous: one avoids attending to x by deciding to concentrate on y, thereby taking advantage of the difficulty of concentrating on more than one thing at a time. It may be that, when this strategy is successful, the unattended input system does indeed get selectively 'switched off', in which case there is a somewhat pickwickian sense in which voluntary control over the operation of an input system is circuitously achieved. Or it may be that the unattended input systems continue to operate but lose their access to some central processes (e.g., to those that mediate storage and report). The latter account is favored, at least for the case of language perception, in light of a fair number of results which seem to show relatively high-level processing of the unattended channel in dichotic listening tasks (Lackner and Garrett, 1973; Corteen and Wood, 1972; Lewis, 1970). But since the experimental results in this area are not univocal, perhaps the most conservative claim is this: input analysis is mandatory in that it provides the *only* route by which transducer outputs can gain access to central processes; if transduced information is to affect thought at all, it must do so via the computations that input systems perform.

I suppose one has to enter a minor caveat. Painters, or so I'm told, learn a little to undo the perceptual constancies and thus to see the world in something like the terms that the retina must deliver—as a two-dimensional spread of color discontinuities varying over time. And it is alleged that phoneticians can be taught to hear their language as something like a sound-stream—viz., as something like what the spikes in the auditory nerves presumably encode. (Though, as a matter of fact, the empirical evidence that phoneticians are actually able to do this is equivocal; see, for example, Lieberman, 1965.) But I doubt that we should take these highly skilled phenomenological reductions very seriously as counterexamples to the generalization that input processes are mandatory. For one thing, precisely because they *are* highly skilled, they may tell us very little about the character of normal perceptual processing. Moreover, it is tendentious—and quite possibly wrong—to think of what painters and phoneticians learn to do as getting access to, as it were, raw transducer output. An at least equally plausible story is that what they learn is how to 'correct' perceptually interpreted representations in ways that compensate for constancy effects. On this latter view, "seeing the visual field" or "hearing the speech stream" are *super*sophisticated perceptual achievements. I don't know which of these stories is the right one, but the issue is clearly empirical and oughtn't to be prejudged.

Anyhow, barring the specialized achievements of painters and phoneticians, one simply cannot see the world under its retinal projection and one has practically no access to the acoustics of utterances in languages that one speaks. (You all know what Swedish and Chinese sound like; what does *English* sound like?) In this respect (and in other respects too, or so I'll presently argue) the input mechanisms approximate the condition often ascribed to reflexes: they are automatically triggered by the stimuli that they apply to. And this is true for both the language comprehension mechanisms and the perceptual systems traditionally so-called.

It is perhaps unnecessary to remark that it does *not* seem to be true for nonperceptual cognitive processes. We have only the narrowest of options about how the objects of perception shall be represented, but we have all the leeway in the world as to how we shall represent the objects of *thought*; outside perception, the way that one deploys one's cognitive resources, is, in general, rationally subservient to one's utilities. Here are some exercises that you can do if you choose: think of *Hamlet* as a revenge play; as a typical product of Mannerist sensibility; as a pot-boiler; as an unlikely vehicle for Greta Garbo. Think of sixteen different ways of using a brick. Think of an utterance of "All Gaul is divided into three parts" as an acoustic object. Now try *hearing* an utterance of "All Gaul is divided into three parts" as an acoustic object. Notice the difference.

No doubt there are *some* limits to the freedom that one enjoys in rationally manipulating the representational capacities of thought. If, indeed, the Freudians are right, more of the direction of thought is mandatory—not to say obsessional—than the uninitiated might suppose. But the quantitative difference surely seems to be there. There is, as the computer people would put it, "executive control" over central representational capacities; and intellectual sophistication consists, in some part, in being able to exert that control in a manner conducive to the satisfaction of one's goals—in ways, in short, that seem likely to get you somewhere. By contrast, perceptual processes apparently apply willy-nilly in disregard of one's immediate concerns. "I couldn't help hearing what you said" is one of those clichés which, often enough, expresses a literal truth; and it is what is *said* that one can't help hearing, not just what is *uttered*.

III.3.   There is only limited central access to the mental representations that input systems compute

It is worth distinguishing the claim that input operations are mandatory (you can't but hear an utterance of a sentence *as* an utterance of a sentence) from the claim that what might be called 'interlevels' of input representation are, typically, relatively inaccessible to consciousness. Not only must you hear an utterance of a sentence as such, but, to a first approximation, you can hear it *only* that way.

What makes this consideration interesting is that, according to all standard theories, the computations that input systems perform typically proceed via the assignment of a number of intermediate analyses of the proximal stimulation. Sentence comprehension, for example, involves not only acoustic encoding but also the recovery of phonetic and lexical content and syntactic form. Apparently an analogous picture applies in the case of vision, where the recognition of a distal array as, say, a-bottle-on-a-table-in-the-corner-of-the-room proceeds via the recovery of a series of preliminary representations (in terms of visual frequencies and primal sketches inter alia. For a review of recent thinking about interlevels of visual representation, see Zucker, 1981).

The present point is that the subject doesn't have equal access to all of these ascending levels of representation—not at least if we take the criterion of accessibility to be the availability for explicit report of the information that these representations encode. Indeed, as I remarked above, the lowest levels (the ones that correspond most closely to transducer outputs) appear to be completely *in*accessible for all intents and purposes. The rule seems to be that, even if perceptual processing goes from 'bottom to top' (each level of representation of a stimulus computed being more abstractly related to transducer outputs than the one that immediately preceded), still *access* goes from top down (the further you get from transducer outputs, the more accessible the representations recovered are to central cognitive systems that presumably mediate conscious report).

A plausible first approximation might be that only such representations as constitute the *final* consequences of input processing are fully and freely available to the cognitive processes that eventuate in the voluntary determination of overt behavior. This arrangement of accessibility relations is reasonable enough assuming, on the one hand, that the computational capacities of central cognitive systems are not inexhaustible in their ability to attend to impinging information and, on the other, that it is the relatively abstract products of input-processing that encode most of the news that we are likely to want to know. I said in section III.2 that the operation of input systems is relatively insensitive to the subject's utilities. By contrast, according to this account, the architectural arrangements that govern exchanges of information between input systems and other mechanisms of cognition do reflect aspects of the organism's standing concerns.

The generalization about the relative inaccessibility of intermediate levels of input analysis is pretty rough, but all sorts of anecdotal and experimental considerations suggest that something of the sort is going on. A well known psychological party trick goes like this:

E: Please look at your watch and tell me the time.
S: (Does so.)
E: Now tell me, without looking again, what is the shape of the numerals on your watch face?
S: (Stumped, evinces bafflement and awe.) (See Morton, 1967)

The point is that visual information which specifies the shape of the numerals must be registered when one reads one's watch, but from the point of view of access to later report, that information doesn't take. One recalls, as it were, pure position with no shape in the position occupied. There are analogous anecdotes to the effect that it is often hard to remember whether somebody you have just been talking to has a beard (or a moustache, or wears glasses). Yet visual information that specifies a beard must be registered and processed whenever you recognize a bearded face. More anecdote: Almost nobody can tell you how the letters and numbers are grouped on a telephone dial, though you use this information whenever you make a phone call. And Nickerson and Adams (1979) have shown that not only are subjects unable to describe a Lincoln penny accurately, they also can't pick out an accurate drawing from ones that get it grossly wrong.

There are quite similar phenomena in the case of language, where it is easy to show that details of syntax (or of the choice of vocabulary) are lost within moments of hearing an utterance, only the gist being retained. (Which did I just say was rapidly lost? Was it the syntactic details or the details of syntax?) Yet it is inconceivable that such information is not registered somewhere in the comprehension process and, within limits, it is possible to enhance its recovery by the manipulation of instructional variables. (For edifying experiments, see Sachs, 1967; Wanner, 1968.)

These sorts of examples make it seem plausible that the relative inaccessibility of lower levels of input analysis is at least in part a matter of how priorities are allocated in the transfer of representations from relatively short- to relatively long-term memory.[18] The idea would be that only quite high-level representations are stored, earlier ones being discarded as soon as subsystems of the input analyzer get the goodness out of them. Or, more precisely, intermediate input representations, when not discarded, are retained only at special cost in memory or attention, the existence of such charges-for-internal-access being itself a prototypical feature of modular systems.

This is, no doubt, part of the story. Witness the fact that in tasks which minimize memory demands by requiring comparison of *simultaneously* presented stimuli, responses that are sensitive to stimulus properties specified at relatively low levels of representation are frequently *faster* than responses to properties of the sort that high-level representations mark. Here, then, the ordering of relative accessibility reverses the top-to-bottom picture proposed above. It may be worth a digression to review some relevant findings.

The classical experimental paradigm is owing to Posner (1978). S's are required to respond 'yes' to visually presented letter pairs when they are *either* font identical (t,t; T,T) *or* alphabetically identical (t,T; T,t). The finding is that when letters in a pair are presented *simultaneously*, response to alphabetically identical pairs that are also font identical is faster than response to pairs that are identical alphabetically but not in font. This effect diminishes asymptotically with increase in the interstimulus interval when the letters are presented *sequentially*.

A plausible (though not mandatory) interpretation is that the representation that specifies the physical shape of the impinging stimulus is computed earlier than representations that specify its alphabetic value. (At a minimum, *some* shape information must be registered prior to alphabetic value, since alphabetic value depends upon shape.) In any event, the fact that representations of shape can drive voluntary responses suggests that they must be available to central processes at *some* point in the course of S's interaction with the stimulus. And this suggests, in turn, that the inaccessibility of font- as compared with alphabetic-information over the relatively long term must be a matter of how memory is deployed rather than of the intrinsic opacity of low-level representations to high-level processes. It looks as though, in these cases, the relative unavailability of lower levels of input analysis is primarily a matter of the way that the subsystems of the input processors interface with memory systems. It is less a matter of information being unconscious than of its being unrecalled. (See also Crowder and Morton, 1969.)

It is unlikely, however, that this is the whole story about the inaccessibility of interlevels of input analysis. For one thing, as was remarked above, some very low levels of stimulus representation appear to be absolutely inaccessible to report. It is, to all intents and purposes (i.e., short of extensive training of the subject) impossible to elicit voluntary responses that are selectively sensitive to subphonetic linguistic distinctions (or, in the case of vision, to parameters of the retinal projection of distal objects) even though we have excellent theoretical grounds for supposing that such information must be registered somewhere in the course of linguistic (/visual) processing. And not *just* theoretical grounds: *we can often show that aspects of the subject's behavior are sensitive to the information that he can't report.*

For example, a famous result on the psychophysics of speech argues that utterances of syllables may be indistinguishable despite very substantial differences in their acoustic structure *so long as these differences are subphonetic.* When, however, quantitatively identical acoustic differences happen to be, as linguists say, 'contrastive'—i.e., when they mark distinctions between phones—they will be quite discriminable to the subject; as distinguishable, say, as "ba" is from "pa". It appears, in short, that there is a perceptual constancy at work which determines, in a wide range of cases, that only such acoustic differences as have linguistic value are accessible to the hearer in discrimination tasks. (See Liberman, et al., 1967.) What is equally striking, however, is that these 'inaccessible' differences *do affect reaction times.* Suppose a/a and a/b are utterance pairs such that the members of the first pair are literally acoustically identical and the members of the second differ only in *non*contrastive acoustic properties—i.e., the acoustic distinction between a and b is subphonetic. As we have seen, it is possible to choose such properties so that the members of the a/b pair are perceptually indistinguishable (as are, of course, the members of the pair a/a).

Even so, in such cases reaction times to make the 'same' judgment for the a/a pair are reliably faster than reaction times to make the 'same' judgment for the a/b pair. (Pisoni and Tash, 1974.) The subject can't report—and presumably can't hear—the difference between signal a and signal b, but his behavior is sensitive to it all the same.

These kinds of cases are legion in studies of the constancies, and this fact bears discussion. The *typical* function of the constancies is to engender perceptual similarity in the face of the variability of proximal stimulation. Proximal variation is very often misleading; the world is, in general, considerably more stable than are its projections onto the surfaces of transducers. Constancies correct for this, so that in general percepts correspond to distal layouts *better than* proximal stimuli do. But, of course, the work of the constancies would be undone unless the central systems which run behavior were required largely to ignore the representations which encode *un*corrected proximal information. The obvious architectural solution is to allow central systems to access information engendered by proximal stimulation only *after* it has been run through the input analyzers. Which is to say that central processes should have free access only to the *outputs* of perceptual processors, interlevels of perceptual processing being correspondingly opaque to higher cognitive systems. This, I'm claiming, is the architecture that we in fact do find.

There appears, in short, to be a generalization to state about input systems as such. Input analysis typically involves *mediated* mappings from transducer outputs onto percepts—mappings that are effected via the computation of interlevels of representation of the impinging stimulus. These intermediate representations are sometimes absolutely inaccessible to central processes, or, in many cases, they are accessible at a price: you can get at them, but only by imposing special demands upon memory or attention. Or, to put it another way: To a first approximation, input systems can be freely queried by memory and other central systems only in respect of *one* of the levels of representation that they compute; and the level that defines this interface is, in general, the one that is most abstractly related to transduced representations. This claim, if true, is substantive; and if, as I believe, it holds for input systems at large, then that is another reason to believe that the construct *input system* subsumes a natural kind.

III.4. Input systems are fast

Identifying sentences and visual arrays are among the fastest of our psychological processes. It is a little hard to quantify this claim because of unclarities about the individuation of mental activities. (What precisely are the boundaries of the processes to be compared? For example, where does sentence (/scene) *recognition* stop and more central activities take over? Compare the discussion in section III.6, below.) Still, granting the imprecision, there are more than enough facts around to shape one's theoretical intuitions.

Among the simplest of voluntary responses are two-choice reactions (push the button if the *left*-hand light goes on). The demands that this task imposes upon the cognitive capacities are minimal, and a practiced subject can respond reliably at latencies on the low side of a quarter of a second. It thus bears thinking about that the recovery of semantic content from a spoken sentence can occur at speeds quite comparable to those achieved in the two-choice reaction paradigm. In particular, appreciable numbers of subjects can 'shadow' continuous speech with a quarter-second latency (shadowing is repeating what you hear as you hear it) and, contrary to some of the original reports, there is now good evidence that such 'fast shadowers' understand what they repeat. (See Marslen-Wilson, 1973.) Considering the amount of processing that must go on in sentence comprehension (unless all our current theories are *totally* wrongheaded), this finding is mind-boggling. And, mind-boggling or otherwise, it is clear that shadowing latency is an extremely conservative measure of the speed of comprehension. Since shadowing requires *repeating* what one is hearing, the 250 msec. of lag between stimulus and response includes not only the time required for the perceptual analysis of the message, but also the time required for the subject's integration of his verbalization.

In fact, it may be that the phenomenon of fast shadowing shows that the efficiency of language processing comes very close to achieving theoretical limits. Since the syllabic rate of normal speech is about 4 per second, the observed 250 msec. latency is compatible with the suggestion that fast shadowers are processing speech in syllable-length units—i.e., that the initiation of the shadower's response is commenced upon the identification of each syllable-length input. Now, work in the psychoacoustics of speech makes it look quite likely that the syllable is the shortest linguistic unit that *can* be reliably identified in the speech stream (see Liberman et al., 1967). Apparently, the acoustic realizations of shorter linguistic forms (like phones) exhibit such extreme context dependence as to make them unidentifiable on a unit-by-unit basis. Only at the level of the syllable do we begin to find stretches of wave form whose acoustic properties are at all reliably related to their linguistic values. If this is so, then it suggests the following profoundly depressing possibility: the responses of fast shadowers lag a syllable behind the stimulus *not* because a quarter second is the upper bound on the speed of the mental processes that mediate language comprehension, but rather because, if the subject were to go any faster, he would overrun the ability of the speech stream to signal linguistic distinctions.[19]

In the attempt to estimate the speed of computation of visual processing, problems of quantification are considerably more severe. On the one hand, the stimulus is not usually spread out in time, so it's hard to determine how much of the input the subject registers before initiating his identificatory response. And, on the other hand, we don't have a taxonomy of visual stimuli comparable to the classification of utterance tokens into linguistic types. Since the question what type a linguistic token belongs to is a great deal clearer than the corresponding question for visual arrays, it is even less obvious in vision than in speech what sort of response should count as indicating that a given array has been identified.

For all of which there is good reason to believe that given a motivated decision about how to quantify the observations, the facts about visual perception would prove quite as appalling as those about language. For example, in one study by Haber (1980), subjects were exposed to 2,560 photographic slides of randomly chosen natural scenes, each slide being exposed for an interval of 10 seconds. Performance on recognition recall (ability to correctly identify a test slide as one that had been seen previously) approached 90 percent one hour after the original exposure. Haber remarks that the results "suggest that recognition of pictures is essentially perfect." Recent work by Potter (personal communication) indicates that 10 seconds of exposure is actually a great deal more than subjects need to effect a perceptual encoding of the stimulus adequate to mediate this near-perfect performance. According to Potter, S's performance in the Haber paradigm asymptotes at an exposure interval of about 2 seconds per slide.

There are some other results of Potter's (1975) that make the point still more graphically. S is shown a sequence of slides of magazine photographs, the rate of presentation of the slides being the experimentally manipulated variable. Prior to each sequence, S is provided with a brief description of an object or event that may appear in one or another slide—e.g., a boat, two men drinking beer, etc. S is to attend to the slides, responding when he sees one that satisfies the description. Under these conditions, S's respond with better than 70 percent accuracy when each slide is exposed for 125 msec. Accuracy asymptotes (at around 96 percent) at exposure times of 167 msec. per slide. It is of some interest that S's are as good at this task as they are at recognition recall (i.e., at making the global judgment that a given slide is one that they have seen before).

Two first-blush morals should be drawn from such findings about the computational efficiency of input processes. First, it contrasts with the relative slowness of paradigmatic central processes like problem-solving; and, second, it is presumably no accident that these very fast psychologicical processes are mandatory.

The first point is, I suppose, intuitively obvious: one can, and often does, spend hours thinking about a problem in philosophy or chess, though there is no reason to suppose that the computational complexity of these problems is greater than that of the ones that are routinely solved effortlessly in the course of perceptual processing. Indeed, the puzzle about input analysis is precisely that the computational complexity of the problem to be solved doesn't seem to predict the difficulty of solving it; or, rather, if it does, the difference between a 'hard' problem and an 'easy' one is measured not in months but in milliseconds. This dissimilarity between perception and thought is surely so adequately robust that it is unlikely to be an artifact of the way that we individuate cognitive achievements. It is only in trick cases, of the sorts that psychologists devise in experimental laboratories, that the perceptual analysis of an utterance or a visual scene is other than effectively instantaneous. What goes on when you parse a standard psycholinguistic poser like "the horse raced past the barn fell" is, almost certainly, *not* the same sort of processing that mediates sentence recognition in the normal case. They even *feel* different.

Second, it may well be that processes of input analysis are fast *because* they are mandatory. Because these processes are automatic, you save computation (hence time) that would otherwise have to be devoted to deciding whether, and how, they ought to be performed. Compare: eyeblink is a fast response *because* it is a reflex—i.e., because you don't have to *decide* whether to blink your eye when someone jabs a finger at it. Automatic responses are, in a certain sense, deeply unintelligent; of the whole range of computational (and, eventually, behavioral) options available to the organism, only a stereotyped subset is brought into play. But what you save by indulging in this sort of stupidity is *not having to make up your mind*, and making your mind up takes time. Reflexes, whatever their limitations, are not in jeopardy of being sicklied o'er with the pale cast of thought. Nor are input processes, according to the present analysis.

There is, however, more than this to be said about the speed of input processes. We'll return to the matter shortly.

III.5. Input systems are informationally encapsulated

Some of the claims that I'm now about to make are in dispute among psychologists, but I shall make them anyway because I think that they are true. I shall run the discussion in this section largely in terms of language, though, as usual, it is intended that the morals should hold for input systems at large.

I remarked above that, almost certainly, understanding an utterance involves establishing its analysis at several different levels of representation: phonetic, phonological, lexical, syntactic, and so forth. Now, in principle, information about the probable structure of the stimulus at any of these levels could be brought to bear upon the recovery of its analysis at any of the others. Indeed, in principle *any* information available to the hearer, including meteorological information, astrological information, or—rather more plausibly—information about the speaker's probable communicative intentions could be brought to bear at any point in the comprehension process. In particular, it is entirely possible that, in the course of computing a structural description, information that is specified only at relatively high levels of representation should be 'fed back' to determine analyses at relatively lower levels.[20] But though this is possible in principle, the burden of my argument is going to be that the operations of input systems are in certain respects unaffected by such feedback.

I want to emphasize the 'in certain respects'. For there exist, in the psychological literature, dramatic illustrations of the effects of information feedback upon some input operations. Consider, for example, the 'phoneme restoration effect' (Warren, 1970). You make a tape recording of a word (as it might be, the word "legislature") and you splice out one of the speech sounds (as it might be, the 's'), which you then replace with a tape recording of a cough. The acoustic structure of the resultant signal is thus /legi(cough)lature/. But what a subject will *hear* when you play the tape to him is an utterance of /legislature/ with a cough 'in the background'. It surely seems that what is going on here is that the perceived phonetic constituency of the utterance is determined not just by the transduced information (not just by information specified at *sub*-phonetic levels of analysis) but also by higher-level information about the probable lexical representation of the utterance (i.e., by the subject's guess that the intended utterance was probably /legislature/).

It is not difficult to imagine how this sort of feedback might be achieved. Perhaps, when the stimulus is noisy, the subject's mental lexicon is searched for a 'best match' to however much of the phonetic content of the utterance has been securely identified. In effect, the lexicon is queried by the instruction 'Find an entry some ten phones long, of which the initial phone sequence is /legi/ and the terminal sequence is /lature/.' The reply to this query constitutes the lexical analysis under which the input is heard.

Apparently rather similar phenomena occur in the case of visual scotoma (where neurological disorders produce a 'hole' in the subject's visual field). The evidence is that scotoma can mask quite a lot of the visual input without creating a phenomenal blind spot for the subject. What happens is presumably that information about higher-level redundancies is fed back to 'fill in' the missing sensory information. Some such process also presumably accounts for one's inability to 'see' one's retinal blind spot.

These sorts of considerations have led to some psychologists (and many theorists in AI) to propose relentlessly top-down models of input analysis, in which the perceptual encoding of a stimulus is determined largely by the subject's (conscious or unconscious) beliefs and expectations, and hardly at all by the stimulus information that transducers provide. Extreme examples of such feedback-oriented approaches can be found in Schank's account of language comprehension, in Neisser's early theorizing about vision, and in 'analysis by synthesis' approaches to sentence parsing. Indeed, a sentimental attachment to what are known generically as 'New Look' accounts of perception (Bruner, 1973) is pervasive in the cognitive science community. It will, however, be a main moral of this discussion that the involvement of certain sorts of feedback in the operation of input systems would be incompatible with their modularity, at least as I propose to construe the modularity thesis. One or other of these doctrines will have to go.

In the long run, which one goes will be a question of how the data turn out. Indeed, a great deal of the empirical interest of the modularity thesis lies in the fact that the experimental predictions it makes tend to be diametrically opposed to the ones that New Look approaches license. But experiments to one side, there are some prima facie reasons for doubting that the computations that input systems perform could have anything like unlimited access to high-level expectations or beliefs. These considerations suggest that even if there are *some* perceptual mechanisms whose operations are extensively subject to feedback, there must be others that compute the structure of a percept largely, perhaps solely, in isolation from background information.

For one thing, there is the widely noted persistence of many perceptual illusions (e.g., the Ames room, the phi phenomenon, the Muller-Lyre illusion in vision; the phoneme restoration and click displacement effects in speech) even in defiance of the subject's explicit knowledge that the percept is illusory. The very same subject who can tell you that the Muller-Lyre arrows are identical in length, who indeed has seen them measured, still finds one looking longer than the other. In such cases it is hard to see an alternative to the view that at least *some* of the background information at the subject's disposal is inaccessible to at least some of his perceptual mechanisms.

An old psychological puzzle provides a further example of this kind. When you move your head, or your eyes, the flow of images across the retina may be identical to what it would be were the head and eyes to remain stationary while the scene moves. So: why don't we experience apparent motion when we move our eyes? Most psychologists now accept one or other version of the "corollary discharge" answer to this problem. According to this story, the neural centers which initiate head and eye motions communicate with the input analyzer in charge of interpreting visual stimulations (See Bizzi, 1968). Because the latter system knows what the former is up to, it is able to discount alterations in the retinal flow that are due to the motions of the receptive organs.

Well, the point of interest for us is that this visual-motor system is informationally encapsulated. Witness the fact that, if you (gently) push your eyeball with your finger (as opposed to moving it in the usual way: by an exercise of the will), you *do* get apparent motion. Consider the moral: when you voluntarily move your eyeball with your finger, you certainly are possessed of the information that it's your eye (and not the visual scene) that is moving. This knowledge is absolutely explicit; if I ask you, you can *say* what's going on. But this explicit information, available to you for (e.g.) report, is *not* available to the analyzer in charge of the perceptual integration of your retinal stimulations. That system has access to corollary discharges from the motor center *and to no other information that you possess.* Modularity with a vengeance.

We've been surveying first blush considerations which suggest that at least some input analyzers are encapsulated with respect to at least some sorts of feedback. The next of these is a point of principle: feedback works only to the extent that the information which perception supplies is redundant; and it *is* possible to perceptually analyze arbitrarily unredundant stimulus arrays. This point is spectacularly obvious in the case of language. If I write "I keep a giraffe in my pocket," you are able to understand me despite the fact that, on even the most inflationary construal of the notion of context, there is nothing in the context of the inscription that would have enabled you to predict either its form or its content. In short, feedback is effective only to the extent that, *prior* to the analysis of the stimulus, the perceiver knows quite a lot about what the stimulus is going to be like. Whereas, the *point* of perception is, surely, that it lets us find out how the world is even when the world is some way that we *don't* expect it to be. The teleology of perceptual capacities presupposes a considerably-less-than-omnis-cient-organism; they'd be no use to God. If you already *know* how things are, why look to *see* how things are?[21]

So: The perceptual analysis of *un*anticipated stimulus layouts (in language and elsewhere) is possible only to the extent that (a) the output of the transducer is insensitive to the beliefs/expectations of the organism; and (b) the input analyzers are adequate to compute a representation of the stimulus from the information that the trans-ducers supply. This is to say that the perception of novelty depends on bottom-to-top perceptual mechanisms.

There is a variety of ways of putting this point, which is, I think, among the most important for understanding the character of the input systems. Pylyshyn (1980) speaks of the "cognitive impen-etrability" of perception, meaning that the output of the perceptual systems is largely insensitive to what the perceiver presumes or desires. Pylyshyn's point is that a condition for the *reliability* of perception, at least for a fallible organism, is that it generally sees what's there, not what it wants or expects to be there. Organisms that don't do so become deceased.

Here is another terminology for framing these issues about the direction of information flow in perceptual analysis: Suppose that the organism is given the problem of determining the analysis of a stimulus at a certain level of representation—e.g., the problem of determining which sequence of words a given utterance encodes. Since, in the general case, transducer outputs underdetermine per-ceptual analyses,[22] we can think of the solution of such problems as involving processes of nondemonstrative inference. In particular, we can think of each input system as a computational mechanism which projects and confirms a certain class of hyputheses on the basis of a certain body of data. In the present example, the available hypotheses are the word sequences that can be constructed from entries in the subject's mental lexicon, and the perceptual problem is to determine which of these sequences provides the right analysis of the currently impinging utterance token. The mechanism which solves the problem is, in effect, the realization of a *confirmation function*: it's a mapping which associates with each pair of a lexical hypothesis and some acoustic datum a value which expresses the degree of confirmation that the latter bestows upon the former. (And similarly, mutatis mutandis, for the nondemonstrative inferences that the other input analyzers effect.) I emphasize that construing the situation this way involves no commitment to a detailed theory of the operation of perceptual systems. *Any* nondemonstrative inference can be viewed as the projection and confirmation of a hypothesis, and I take it that perceptual inferences must in general be nondemonstrative, since their underdetermination by sensory data is not in serious dispute.

Looked at this way, the claim that input systems are informationally encapsulated is equivalent to the claim that the data that can bear on the confirmation of perceptual hypotheses includes, in the general case, considerably less than the organism may know. That is, the confirmation function for input systems does not have access to all of the information that the organism internally represents; there are restrictions upon the allocation of internally represented information to input processes.

Talking about the direction of information flow in psychological processes and talking about restrictions upon the allocation of information to such processes are thus two ways of talking about the same thing. If, for example, we say that the flow of information in language comprehension runs directly from the determination of the phonetic structure of an utterance to the determination of its lexical content, then we are saying that only phonetic information is available to whatever mechanism decides the level of confirmation of perceptual hypotheses about lexical structure. On that account, such mechanisms are encapsulated with respect to *non*phonetic information; they have no access to such information; not even if it is *internally represented, accessible to other cognitive processes* (i.e., to cognitive processes other than the assignment of lexical analyses to phone sequences) and *germane* in the sense that if it *were* brought to bear in lexical analysis, it would affect the confirmation levels of perceptual hypotheses about lexical structure.

I put the issue of informational encapsulation in terms of constraints on the data available for hypothesis confirmation because doing so will help us later, when we come to compare input systems with central cognitive processes. Suffice it to say, for the moment, that this formulation suggests another possible reason why input systems are so fast. We remarked above that the computations that input systems perform are mandatory, and that their being so saves time that would otherwise have to be used in executive decision-making. We now add that input systems are bull-headed and that this, too, makes for speed. The point is this: to the extent that input systems are informationally encapsulated, of all the information that might *in principle* bear upon a problem of perceptual analysis only a portion (perhaps only quite a small and stereotyped portion) is actually admitted for consideration. This is to say that speed is purchased for input systems by permitting them to ignore lots of the facts. Ignoring the facts is not, of course, a good recipe for problem-solving in the general case. But then, as we have seen, input systems don't function in the *general* case. Rather, they function to provide very special kinds of representations of very specialized inputs (to pair transduced representations with formulas in the domains of central processes). What operates in the general case, and what is sensitive, at least in principle, to *everything* that the organism knows, are the central processes themselves. Of which more later.

I should add that these reflections upon the value of bull-headedness do not, as one might suppose, entirely depend upon assumptions about the speed of memory search. Consider an example. Ogden Nash once offered the following splendidly sane advice: "If you're called by a panther/don't anther." Roughly, we want the perceptual identification of panthers to be very fast and to err, if at all, only on the side of false positives. If there is a body of information that must be deployed in such perceptual identifications, then we would prefer not to have to recover that information from a large memory, assuming that the speed of access varies inversely with the amount of information that the memory contains. This is a way of saying that we do not, on that assumption, want to have to access panther-identification information from the (presumably *very* large) central storage in which representations of background-information-at-large are generally supposed to live. Which is in turn to say that we don't want the input analyzer that mediates panther identification to communicate with the central store on the assumption that large memories are searched slowly.

Suppose, however, that random access to a memory is *in*sensitive to its size. *Even so* panther-identification (and, mutatis mutandis, other processes of input analysis) had better be insensitive to much of what one knows. Suppose that we can get at *everything* we know about panthers *very fast*. We still have the problem of deciding, for each such piece of information retrieved from memory, *how much inductive confirmation it bestows upon the hypothesis that the presently observed black-splotch-in-the-visual-field is a panther.* The point is that in the rush and scramble of panther identification, there are many things I know about panthers whose bearing on the likely pantherhood of the present stimulus *I do not wish to have to consider.* As, for example, that my grandmother abhors panthers; that every panther bears some distant relation to my Siamese cat Jerrold J.; that there are no panthers on Mars; that there is an Ogden Nash poem about panthers . . . etc. Nor is this all; for, in fact, the property of being 'about panthers' is not one that can be surefootedly relied upon. Given enough context, practically everything I know can be construed as panther related; and, *I do not want to have to consider everything I know* in the course of perceptual panther iden- tification. In short, the point of the informational encapsulation of input processes is not—or not solely—to reduce the memory space that must be searched to find information that is perceptually rel- evant. The primary point is to so restrict the number of *confirmation relations* that need to be estimated as to make perceptual identi- fications fast. (I am indebted to Scott Fahlman for raising questions that provoked the last two paragraphs.)[23]

The informational encapsulation of the input systems is, or so I shall argue, the essence of their modularity. It's also the essence of the analogy between the input systems and reflexes; reflexes are informationally encapsulated with bells on.

Suppose that you and I have known each other for many a long year (we were boys together, say) and you have come fully to appreciate the excellence of my character. In particular, you have come to know perfectly well that under no conceivable circum- stances would I stick my finger in your eye. Suppose that this belief of yours is both explicit and deeply felt. You would, in fact, go to the wall for it. Still, if I jab my finger near enough to your eyes, and fast enough, you'll blink. To say, as we did above, that the blink reflex is mandatory is to say, inter alia, that it has no access to what you know about my character or, for that matter, to any other of your beliefs, utilities and expectations. For this reason the blink reflex is often produced when sober reflection would show it to be uncalled for; like panther-spotting, it is prepared to trade false positives for speed.

That is what it is like for a psychological system to be informationally encapsulated. If you now imagine a system that is encapsulated in the way that reflexes are, but also computational in a way that reflexes are not, you will have some idea of what I'm proposing that input systems are like.

It is worth emphasizing that being modular in this sense is not quite the same thing as being autonomous in the sense that Gall had in mind. For Gall, if I read him right, the claim that the vertical faculties are autonomous was practically equivalent to the claim that there are no horizontal faculties for them to share. Musical aptitude, for example, is autonomous *in that* judging musical ideas shares no cognitive mechanisms with judging mathematical ideas; remembering music shares no cognitive mechanisms with remembering faces; perceiving music shares no cognitive mechanisms with perceiving speech; and so forth.

Now, it is unclear to what extent the input systems *are* autonomous in *that* sense. We do know, for example, that there are systematic relations between the amount of computational strain that decoding a sentence places on the language handling systems and the subject's ability to perform simultaneous nonlinguistic tasks quickly and accurately. 'Phoneme monitor' (Foss, 1970) techniques, and others, can be used to measure such interactions, and the results suggest a picture that is now widely accepted among cognitive psychologists: Mental processes often compete for access to resources variously characterized as attention, short-term memory, or work space; and the result of allocating such resources to one of the competing processes is a decrement in the performance of the others. How general this sort of interaction is is unclear in the present state of the art (for contrary cases, suggesting isolated work spaces for visual imagery on the one hand and verbal recall on the other, see Brooks, 1968). In any event, where such competition does obtain, it is a counterexample to autonomy in what I am taking to be Gall's understanding of that notion.[24]

On the other hand, we can think of autonomy in a rather different way from Gall's—viz., in terms of informational encapsulation. So, instead of asking what access language processes (e.g.) have to *computational resources* that other systems also share, we can ask what access they have to the *information* that is available to other systems. If we do look at things this way, then the question "how much autonomy?" is the same question as "how much constraint on information flow?" In a nutshell: one way that a system can be autonomous is by being encapsulated, by not having access to facts that other systems know about. I am claiming that, whether or not the input systems are autonomous in Gall's sense, they are, to an interesting degree, autonomous in this informational sense.

However, I have not yet given any arguments (except some impressionistic ones) to show that the input systems actually are informationally encapsulated. In fact, I propose to do something considerably more modest: I want to suggest some caveats that ought to be, but frequently aren't, observed in interpreting the sorts of data that have usually been alleged in support of the contrary view. I think that many of the considerations that have seemed to suggest that input processes are cognitively penetrable—that they are importantly affected by the subject's belief about context, or his background information, or his utilities—are, in fact, equivocal or downright misleading. I shall therefore propose several ground rules for evaluating claims about the cognitive penetrability of input systems; and I'll suggest that, when these rules are enforced, the evidence for 'New Look' approaches to perception begins to seem not impressive. My impulse in all this is precisely analogous to what Marr and Pogio say motivates their work on vision: ". . . to examine ways of squeezing the last ounce of information from an image before taking recourse to the descending influence of high-level interpretation on early processing" (1977, pp. 475–476).

(a) Nobody doubts that the information that input systems provide must somehow be reconciled with the subject's background knowledge. We sometimes know that the world can't really be the way that it looks, and such cases may legitimately be described as the correction of input analyses by top-down information flow. (This, ultimately, is the reason for refusing to identify input analysis with perception. The point of perception is the fixation of belief, and the fixation of belief is a *conservative* process—one that is sensitive, in a variety of ways, to what the perceiver already knows. Input analysis may be informationally encapsulated, but perception surely is not.) However, to demonstrate *that* sort of interaction between input analyses and background knowledge is not, in and of itelf, tantamount to demonstrating the cognitive penetrability of the former; you need also to show that the locus of the top-down effect is *internal* to the input system. That is, you need to show that the information fed back interacts with interlevels of input-processing and not merely with the final results of such processing. The penetrability of a system is, by definition, its susceptibility to top-down effects at stages *prior* to its production of output.

I stress this point because it seems quite possible that input systems specify only relatively shallow levels of representation (see the next section). For example, it is quite possible that the perceptual representation delivered for a token sentence specifies little more than the type to which the token belongs (and hence does *not* specify such information as the speech act potential of the token, still less the speech act performed by the tokening). If this is so, then data showing effects of the hearer's background information on, e.g., his estimates of the speaker's communicative intentions would *not* constitute evidence for the cognitive penetration of the presumptive language-comprehension module; by hypothesis, the computations involved in making such estimates would not be among those that the language-comprehension module *per se* performs. Similarly, mutatis mutandis, in the case of vision. There is a great deal of evidence for context effects upon certain aspects of visual object recognition. But such evidence counts for nothing in the present discussion unless there is independent reason to believe that these aspects of object recognition are part of visual input analysis. Perhaps the input system for vision specifies the stimulus only in terms of "primal sketches" (for whose cognitive impenetrability there is, by the way, some nontrivial evidence. See Marr and Nishihara (1978).) The problem of assessing the degree of informational encapsulation of input systems is thus not independent of the problem of determining how such systems are individuated and what sorts of representations constitute their outputs. I shall return to the latter issue presently; for the moment, I'm just issuing caveats.

(b) Evidence for the cognitive penetrability of some computational mechanism that does what input systems do is not, in and of itself, evidence for the cognitive penetrability of input systems.

To see what is at issue here, consider some of the kinds of findings that have been taken as decisively exhibiting the effects of background expectations upon language perception. A well known way of estimating such expectations is the use of the so-called Cloze procedure. Roughly, S is presented with the first n words of a sentence and is asked to complete the fragment. Favored completions (as, for example, "salt" in the case of the fragment "I have the pepper, but would you please pass the ————") are said to be "high Cloze" and are assumed to indicate what the subject would expect a speaker to say next if he had just uttered a token of the fragment. An obvious generalization allows the estimation of the Cloze value at each point in a sentence, thereby permitting experiments in which the average Cloze value of the stimulus sentences is a manipulated variable.

It is quite easy to show that relative Cloze value affects S's per- ← formance on a number of experimental tasks, and it is reasonable to infer from such demonstrations that whatever mechanisms mediate the performance of these tasks must have access to S's expectations about what speakers are likely to say, hence not just to the 'stimulus' (e.g., acoustic) properties of the linguistic token under analysis. (For an early review of the literature on redundancy effects in sentence processing, see Miller and Isard, 1963.) So, for example, it can be shown that the accuracy of S's perception of sentences heard under masking noise is intimately related to the average Cloze value of the sentences: high Cloze sentences can be understood under conditions of greater distortion than the perception of low Cloze sentences tolerates. (Similarly, high Cloze sentences are, in general, more easily remembered than low Cloze sentences; recognition thresholds for words that are high Cloze in a context are lower than those for words that are low Cloze in that context; and so forth.)

The trouble with such demonstrations, however, is that although they show that there exist *some* language-handling processes that have access to the hearer's expectations about what is likely to be said, they do *not* show that the input systems enjoy such access. For example, it might be argued that, in situations where the stimulus is acoustically degraded, the subject is, in effect, encouraged to guess the identity of the material that he can't hear. (Similarly, mutatis mutandis, in memory experiments where a reasonable strategy for the subject is to guess at such of the material as he can't recall.) Not surprisingly, in such circumstances, the subject's background information comes into play with measurable effect. The question, however, is whether the psychological mechanisms deployed in the slow, relatively painful, highly attentional process of reconstructing noisy or otherwise degraded linguistic stimuli are the same mechanisms which mediate the automatic and fluent processes of normal speech perception.

That this question is not merely frivolous is manifested by results such as those of Fishler and Bloom (1980). Using a task in which sentences are presented in clear, they found only a marginal effect of high Cloze on the recognition of test words, and such effects vanished entirely when the stimuli were presented at high rates. (High presentation rates presumably discourage guessing; guessing takes time.) By contrast, words that are 'semantically anomalous' in context showed considerable inhibition in comparison with neutral controls. This last finding is of interest because it suggests that at least some of the effects of sentence context in speech recognition must be, as psychologists sometimes put it, 'post-perceptual'. In our terminology, these processes must operate *after* the input system has provided a (tentative) analysis of the lexical content of the stimulus. The point is that even if the facilitation of redundant items is mediated by predictive, expectation-driven mechanisms, the inhibition of contextually anomalous items cannot be. It is arguable that, in the course of speech perception, one is forever making such predictions as that 'pepper' will occur in 'salt and ----; but surely one can't also be forever predicting that 'dog', 'tomorrow', and all the other anomalous expressions will *not* occur there.[25] The moral is: some processes which eventuate in perceptual identifications are, doubtless, cognitively penetrated. But this is compatible with the informational encapsulation of the input systems themselves. Some traditional enthusiasm for context-driven perceptual models may have been prompted by confusion on this point.

(c) The claim that input systems are informationally encapsulated must be very carefully distinguished from the claim that there is top-down information flow *within* these systems. These issues are very often run together, with consequent exaggeration of the well-groundedness of the case against encapsulation.

Consider, once again, the phoneme restoration effect. Setting aside the general caution that experiments with distorted stimuli provide dubious grounds for inferences about speech perception in clear, phoneme restoration provides considerable prima facie evidence that phone identification has access to what the subject knows about the lexical inventory of his language. If this interpretation is correct, then phoneme restoration illustrates top-down information flow in speech perception. It does *not*, however, illustrate the cognitive penetrability of the language input system. To show that that system is penetrable (hence informationally unencapsulated), you would have to show that its processes have access to information that is not specified at any of the levels of representation that the language input system computes; for example, that it has generalized access to what the hearer knows about the probable beliefs and intentions of his interlocutors. If, by contrast, the 'background information' deployed in phoneme restoration is simply the hearer's knowledge of the words in his language, then that counts as top-down flow within the language module; on any remotely plausible account, the knowledge of a language includes knowledge of its lexicon.

The most recent work in phoneme restoration makes this point with considerable force. Samuel (1981) has shown that both information about the lexical inventory and 'semantic' information supplied by sentential context affect the magnitude of the phoneme restoration effect. Specifically, you get more restoration in words than in (phonologically possible) nonwords, and you get more restoration when a word is predictable in sentence context than when the context is neutral. This looks like the penetration of phone recognition by both lexical and 'background' information, but the appearance is misleading. In fact, Samuel's data suggest that, of the two effects, *only the former* is strictly perceptual, the latter operating in consequence of a response bias to report predictable words as intact. (Detection theoretically: the word/nonword difference affects d', whereas the neutral context/predictive context difference affects β.) As Samuel points out, the amount of restoration is inversely proportional to S's ability to distinguish the stimulus word with a phone missing from an undistorted token of the same type; and, on Samuel's data, this discrimination is actually *better* for items that are highly predictable in context than for items that aren't. Another case, in short, where what had been taken to be an example of context-driven prediction in perception is, in fact, an effect of the biasing of post-perceptual decision processes.

The importance of distinguishing cognitive penetration from intramodular effects can be seen in many other cases where predictive analysis in perception is demonstrable. It is, for example, probable (though harder to show than one might have supposed) that top-down processes are involved in the identification of the surface constituent structure of sentences (see Wright, 1982). For example, it appears that the identification of nouns is selectively facilitated in contexts like T A ──────, the identification of verbs is selectively facilitated in contexts like T N ──────, and so forth. Such facilitation indicates that the procedures for assigning lexical items to form classes have access to information about the general conditions upon the well-formedness of constituent structure trees.

Now, it is a question of considerable theoretical interest whether, and to what extent, predictive analysis plays a role in parsing; but this issue must be sharply distinguished from the question whether the parser is informationally encapsulated. Counterexamples to encapsulation must exhibit the sensitivity of the parser to information that is not specified internal to the language-recognition module, and constraints on syntactic well-formedness are paradigms of information that does *not* satisfy this condition. The issue is currently a topic of intensive experimental and theoretical inquiry; but as things stand I know of *no* convincing evidence that syntactic parsing is ever guided by the subject's appreciation of semantic context or of 'real world' background. Perhaps this is not surprising; there are, in general, so many syntactically different ways of saying the same thing that even if context allowed you to estimate the *content* of what is about to be said, that information wouldn't much increase your ability to predict its *form*.[26]

These questions about where the interacting information comes from (whether it comes from inside or outside the input system) take on a special salience in light of the following consideration: it is possible to imagine ways in which mechanisms *internal* to a module might contrive to, as it were, mimic effects of cognitive penetration. The operation of such mechanisms might thus invite overestimations of the extent to which the module has access to the organism's general informational resources. To see how this might occur, let's return to the question of contextual facilitation of word recognition; traditionally a parade case for New Look theorizing, but increasingly an area in which the data are coming to seem equivocal.

Here are the bare bones of an ingenious experiment of David Swinney's (1979; for further, quite similar, results, see Tannenhaus, Leirnau, and Seidenberg, 1979). The subject listens to a stimulus sentence along the lines of "Because he was afraid of electronic surveillance, the spy carefully searched the room for bugs." Now, we know from previous research that the response latencies for 'bugs' (say, in a word/nonword decision task) will be faster in this context, where it is relatively predictable, than in a neutral context where it is acceptable but relatively low Cloze. This seems to be— and is traditionally taken to be—the sort of result which demonstrates how expectations based upon an intelligent appreciation of sentential context can guide lexical access; the subject predicts 'bugs' before he hears the word. His responses are correspondingly accelerated whenever his prediction proves true. Hence, cognitive penetration of lexical access.

You can, or so it seems, gild this lily. Suppose that, instead of measuring reaction time for word/nonword decisions on 'bugs', you simultaneously present (flashed on a screen that the subject can see) a different word belonging to the same (as one used to say) 'semantic field' (e.g., 'microphones'). If the top-down story is right in supposing that the subject is using semantic/background information to predict lexical content, then 'microphones' is as good a prediction in context as 'bugs' is, so you might expect that 'microphones', too, will exhibit facilitation as compared with a neutral context. And so it proves to do. Cognitive penetration of lexical access with bells on, or so it would appear.

But the appearance is misleading. For Swinney's data show that if you test with 'insects' instead of 'microphones', you get the same result: facilitation as compared with a neutral context. Consider what this means. 'Bugs' has two paraphrases: 'microphones' and 'insects'. But though only one of these is contextually relevant, *both are contextually facilitated*. This looks a lot less like the intelligent use of contextual/background information to guide lexical access. What it looks like instead is some sort of associative relation among lexical forms (between, say, 'spy' and 'bug'); a relation pitched at a level of representation sufficiently superficial to be *in*sensitive to the semantic content of the items involved. This possibility is important for the following reason: If facilitation is mediated by merely interlexical relations (and not by the interaction of background information with the semantic content of the item and its context), then the information that is exploited to produce the facilitation can be represented *in the lexicon*; hence *internal to the language recognition module*. And if that is right, then contextual facilitation of lexical access is *not* an argument for the cognitive penetration of the module. It makes a difference, as I remarked above, where the penetrating information comes from.

Let's follow this just a little further. Suppose the mental lexicon is a sort of connected graph, with lexical items at the nodes and with paths from each item to several others. We can think of accessing an item in the lexicon as, in effect, exciting the corresponding node; and we can assume that one of the consequences of accessing a node is that excitation spreads along the pathways that lead from it. Assume, finally, that when excitation spreads through a portion of the lexical network, response thresholds for the excited nodes are correspondingly lowered. Accessing a given lexical item will thus decrease the response times for items to which it is connected. (This picture is familiar from the work of, among others, Morton, 1969, and Collins and Loftus, 1975; for relevant experimental evidence, see Meyer and Schvaneveldt, 1971.)

The point of the model-building is to suggest how mechanisms internal to the language processor could mimic the effects that cognitive penetration would produce if the latter indeed occurred. In the present example, what mimics the background knowledge that (roughly) spies have to do with bugs is the existence of a connection betweeen the node assigned to the word 'spy' and the node assigned to the word 'bug'. Facilitation of 'bug' in spy contexts is affected by the excitation of such intralexical connections.

Why should these intralexical connections exist? Surely not just in order to lead psychologists to overestimate the cognitive penetrability of language-processing. In fact, if one works the other way 'round and assumes that the input systems are encapsulated, one might think of the mimicry of penetration as a way that the input processors contrive to make the best of their informational isolation. Presumably, what encapsulation buys is speed; and, as we remarked above, it buys speed at the price of unintelligence. It would, one supposes, take a lot of time to make reliable decisions about whether there is the kind of relation between spies and bugs that makes it on balance likely that the current token of 'spy' will be followed by a token of 'bug'. But that is precisely the kind of decision that the subject would have to make if the contextual facilitation of lexical access were indeed an effect of background knowledge interacting with the semantic content of the context. The present suggestion is that no such intelligent evaluation of the options takes place; there is merely a brute facilitation of the recognition of 'bug' consequent upon the recognition of 'spy'. The condition of this brute facilitation buying anything is that it should be possible, with reasonable accuracy, to mimic what one knows about connectedness *in the world* by establishing corresponding connections among entries in the mental lexicon. In effect, the strategy is to use the structure of interlexical connections to mimic the structure of knowledge. The mimicry won't be precise (a route from 'spy' to 'insect' will be generated as a by-product of the route from 'spy' to 'bug'). But there's no reason to doubt that it may produce savings over all.

Since we are indulging speculations, we might as well indulge this one: It is a standing mystery in psychology why there should be interlexical associations at all; why subjects should exhibit a reliable and robust disposition to associate 'salt' with 'pepper', 'cat' with 'dog', 'mother' with 'father', and so forth. In the heyday of associationism, of course, such facts seemed quite *un*mysterious; they were, indeed, the stuff of which the mental life was supposed to be made. On one account the utterance of a sentence was taken to be a chained response, and associations among lexical items were what held the links together. According to still earlier tradition, the postulation of associative connections between Ideas was to be the mechanism for reconstructing the notion of degree of belief. None of this seems plausible now, however. Belief is a matter (not of association but) of *judgment*; sentence production is a matter (not of association but) of *planning*. So, what on earth are associations *for*?

The present suggestion is that associations are the means whereby stupid processing systems manage to behave as though they were smart ones. In particular, interlexical associations are the means whereby the language processor is enabled to act as though it knows that spies have to do with bugs (whereas, in fact, it knows no such thing). The idea is that, just as the tradition supposed, terms for things frequently connected in experience become themselves connected in the lexicon. Such connection is *not* knowledge; it is not even judgment. It is simply the mechanism of the contextual adjustment of response thresholds. Or, to put the matter somewhat metaphysically, the formation of interlexical connections buys the synchronic encapsulation of the language processor at the price of its cognitive penetrability *across time*. The information one has about how things are related in the world is inaccessible to modulate lexical access; that is what the encapsulation of the language processor implies. But one's experience of the relations of things in the world does affect the structure of the lexical network—viz., by instituting connections among lexical nodes. If the present line of speculation is correct, these connections have a real, if modest, role to play in the facilitation of the perceptual analysis of speech. The traditional, fundamental, and decisive objection to association is that it is too stupid a relation to form the basis of a mental life. But stupidity, when not indulged in to excess, is a virtue in fast, peripheral processes; which is exactly what I have been supposing input processes to be.

I am not quite claiming that all the putative effects of information about background (context, etc.) on sentence recognition are artifacts of connections in the lexical network (though, as a matter of fact, such experimental attempts as I've seen to demonstrate a residual effect of context after interlexical/associative factors are controlled for strike me as not persuasive). I am claiming only that the possibility of such artifacts contaminates quite a lot of the evidence that is standardly alleged. The undoubted fact that "semantically" coherent text is relatively easy to process does not, in and of itself, demonstrate that the input system for language has access to what the organism knows about how the world coheres. Such experimental evidence as supported early enthusiasms for massively top-down perceptual models was, I think, sexy but inconclusive; and the possibility of a modular treatment of input processes provides motivation for its reconsideration. The situation would seem to be paradigmatically Kuhnian: the data look different to a jaundiced eye.

Consider the provenance of New Look theorizing. Cognitive psychologists in the '40s and '50s were faced with the proposal that perception is *literally* reflexive; for example, that the theory of perception is reducible without residue to the theory of discriminative operant response. It was natural and admirable in such circumstances to stress the 'intelligence' of perceptual integration. However, in retrospect it seems that the intelligence of perceptual integration may have been seriously misconstrued by those who were most its partisans.

In the ideal condition—one approached more frequently in the textbooks than *in rerum naturae*, to be sure—reflexes have two salient properties. They are computationally simple (the stimulus is "directly connected" to the response), and they are informationally encapsulated (see above). I'm suggesting that New Look theories failed to distinguish these properties. They thus assumed, wrongly, that the disanalogy between perceptual and reflexive processes consisted in the capacity of the former to access and exploit background information. From the point of view of the modularity thesis, this is a case of the right intuition leading to the wrong claim. Input systems *are* computationally elaborated. Their typical function is to perform inference-like operations on representations of impinging stimuli. Processes of input analysis are thus unlike reflexes in respect of the character and complexity of the operations that they perform. But this is quite compatible with reflexes and input processes being similar in respect of their informational encapsulation; in this latter respect, both of them contrast with "central processes"—problem-solving and the like—of which cognitive penetrability is perhaps the most salient feature, or so I shall argue below. To see that informational encapsulation and computational elaboration are compatible properties, it is only necessary to bear in mind that unencapsulation is the exploitation of information from *outside* a system; a computationally elaborated sytem can thus be encapsulated if it stores the information that its computations exploit. Encapsulation is a matter of foreign affairs; computational elaboration begins at home.

It may be useful to summarize this discussion of the informational encapsulation of input systems by comparing it with some recent, and very interesting, suggestions owing to the philosopher Steven Stich (1978). Stich's discussion explores the difference between belief and the epistemic relation that is alleged to hold between, for example, speaker/hearers and the grammar of their native language (the relation that Chomsky calls 'cognizing'). Stich supposes, for purposes of argument, that the empirical evidence shows that speakers *in some sense* 'know' the grammar of their native language; his goal is to say something about what that sense is.

Let us call the epistemic relation that a native speaker has to the grammar of his language *subdoxastic* belief.[27] Stich suggests that there are two respects in which subdoxastic beliefs differ from beliefs strictly so-called. In the first place, as practically everybody has emphasized, subdoxastic beliefs are *unconscious*. But, Stich adds, subdoxastic beliefs are also typically "inferentially unintegrated." The easiest way to understand what Stich means by this is to consider one of his examples.

> If a linguist believes a certain generalization to the effect that no transformation rule exhibits a certain characteristic, and if he comes to (nonsubdoxastically) believe a given transformation which violates the generalization, he may well infer that the generalization is false. But merely having the rule stored (in the way that we are assuming all speakers of the language do) does not enable the linguist to draw the inference. . . . Suppose that for some putative rule, you have come to believe that if r then Chomsky is seriously mistaken. Suppose further that, as it happens, r is in fact among the rules stored by your language processing mechanism. The belief along with the subdoxastic state will not lead to the belief that Chomsky is seriously mistaken. By contrast, if you believe (perhaps even mistakenly) that r, then the belief that Chomsky is seriously mistaken is likely to be inferred. [pp. 508–509]

Or, as Stich puts the argument at another point, "It is characteristic of beliefs that they generate further beliefs via inference. What is more, beliefs are inferentially promiscuous. Provided with a suitable set of supplementary beliefs, almost any belief can play a role in the inference to any other. . . . (However) subdoxastic states, as contrasted with beliefs, are largely inferentially isolated from the large body of inferentially integrated beliefs to which a subject has (conscious) access."

Now, as Stich clearly sees, the proposal that subdoxastic states are typically both unconscious and inferentially unintegrated raises a question—viz., *Why should these two properties co-occur?* Why should it be, to put it in my terminology, that subdoxastic states are typically encapsulated with respect to the processes which affect the inferential integration of beliefs?

Notice that there is a kind of encapsulation that follows from unconsciousness: an unconscious belief cannot play a role as a premise in the sort of reasoning that goes on in the conscious drawing of inferences. Stich is, however, urging something more interesting than this trivial truth. Stich's claim is that subdoxastic beliefs are largely inaccessible even to *un*conscious mental processes of belief fixation. If this claim is true, the question does indeed arise why it should be so.

I want to suggest, however, that the question doesn't arise because, as a matter of act, subdoxastic beliefs are not in general encapsulated; or, to put it more precisely, they are not in general encapsulated *qua* subdoxastic. Consider, as counterexamples, one's subdoxastic views about inductive and deductive warrant; for example, one's subdoxastic acquiescence in the rule of *modus ponens*. On the sort of psychological theory that Stich has in mind, subdoxastic knowledge of such principles must be accessible to practically all mental processes, since practically all inferential processes exploit them in one way or another. One's subdoxastic beliefs about validity and confirmation are thus quite unlike one's subdoxastic beliefs about the rules of grammar; though both are unconscious, the former are paradigms of promiscuous and unencapsulated mental states. So the connection between unconsciousness and encapsulation cannot be *intrinsic*.

Nevertheless, I think that Stich is onto something important. For, though much unconscious information must be widely accessible to processes of fixation of belief, it is quite true that very many of the examples of unconscious beliefs for which there is currently good empirical evidence are encapsulated. This is because most of our current cognitive science is the science of input systems, and, as we have seen, *informational encapsulation is arguably a pervasive feature of such systems.* Input systems typically do not exchange subdoxastic information with central processes or with one another.

Stich almost sees this point. He says that "subdoxastic states occur in a variety of separate, special purpose cognitive systems" (p. 508). True enough; but they must also occur in integrated, general purpose systems (in what I'm calling "central" systems), assuming that much of the fixation of belief is both unconscious and subserved by inferential mechanisms of that kind. The point is: subdoxastic states are informationally encapsulated *only* insofar as they are states of special purpose systems (e.g., states of input analyzers). Practically all psychologically interesting cognitive states are unconscious; but it is only the beliefs accessible to modules that are subdoxastic by the second of Stich's criteria as well.

III.6.   Input analyzers have 'shallow' outputs.

The question where to draw the line between observation and inference (in the psychological version, between perception and cognition) is one of the most vexed, and most pregnant, in the philosophy of science. One finds every opinion from the extreme 'foundationalist' view, which restricts observation to processes that issue in infallible introspective reports, to the recent revisionism which denies that the distinction is in any respect principled. (Hanson, 1958, for example, holds that a physicist can *see* that the cloud chamber contains a proton track in the same sense of 'see' that is operative when Smith sees that there's a spot on Jones' tie.) Sometimes the argument for this sort of view is based explicitly on accounts of perception borrowed from New Look psychology, which suggests that *all* perception is ineliminably and boundlessly theory laden; see Goodman (1978).

Philosophers have cared about the observation/inference distinction largely for epistemological reasons; what is (nondemonstratively) inferred is supposed to run an inductive risk from which what is observed is supposed to be free. And it has seemed important to some epistemologists that whatever count as the data statements of a science should be isolated from such risk, the idea being that unless some contingent truths are certain, no empirical theory can compel rational belief.

I am not myself much moved by the idea that inductive warrant is inherited upward in science from a base level of indubitable truths; and barring some such assumption, the philosophical problem of making the observation/theory distinction rigorous seems less consequent than was once supposed. However, the corresponding psychological problem of saying where perceptual processes interface with cognitive ones must be addressed by anyone who takes the postulation of modular input systems seriously. For one thing, it is a point of definition that distinct functional components cannot interface *everywhere* on pain of their ceasing to be distinct. It is this consideration that flow-chart notation captures by drawing boxes around the processing systems it postulates. That only the inputs and outputs of functionally individuated systems can mediate their information exchanges is tautological.

Moreover, we have seen that the plausibility of claims for the informational encapsulation of an input system depends very much on how one draws the distinction between its *outputs* and its *interlevels* of representation. Since it is common ground that there must be *some* mental processes in which perception interacts with background knowledge and with utilities, the issue about informational encapsulation is whether such interactions take place *internal* to the input systems. But the question what is internal to a system, and the question what is to count as the output of the system, are patently two ways of asking the same thing.

In general, the more constrained the information that the outputs of perceptual systems are assumed to encode—the shallower their outputs, the more plausible it is that the computations that effect the encoding are encapsulated. If, for example, the visual analysis system can report only upon the shapes and colors of things (all higher-level integrations being post-perceptual) it is correspondingly plausible that all the information that system exploits may be represented internal to it. By contrast, if the visual system can deliver news about protons (as a psychologized version of the Hanson story would suggest), then the likelihood that visual analysis is informationally encapsulated is negligible. Chat about protons surely implies free access to quite a lot of what I have been calling 'background knowledge'.

In this section I want to make a few, highly speculative suggestions about how the outputs of the language and visual processors might be characterized—that is, about the level of representation at which these systems interface with central processes. I shall rely heavily on the assumptions that input computations are very fast, and that their outputs are typically phenomenologically salient (see above). Consonant with these assumptions, I shall argue that there are some reasonable proposals to make about how to distinguish visual and linguistic perception from the cognitive processes with which they interface. It turns out, however, that there is nothing *episte-*

mologically special about the levels of representation which constitute the outputs of the visual (/linguistic) processing mechanisms. So if, in the spirit of epistemology naturalized, one leaves it to psychologists to draw the observation/theory distinction, then, according to these proposals, there is nothing epistemologically interesting about that distinction. For example, it does *not* correspond to the distinction between what we infallibly know and what we merely justifiably surmise. This seems to me, if anything, to argue in favor of drawing the line where I propose to draw it; still this version of naturalized epistemology may strike some epistemologists as far too deflationary.

What representation of an utterance does the language input processor compute? Or, to put the question in the context of the preceding discussion, which phenomenologically accessible properties of an utterance are such that, on the one hand, their recovery is mandatory, fast, and relevant to the perceptual encoding of the utterance and, on the other, such that their recovery might be achieved by an informationally encapsulated computational mechanism? Clearly, there is a wide choice of properties of utterances that *could* be computed by computational systems whose access to background information is, in one way or another, interestingly constrained—the duration of the utterance, e.g. For all that, there is, in the case of language, a glaringly obvious galaxy of candidates for modular treatment—viz., those properties that utterances have in virtue of some or other aspects of their linguistic structure (where this means, mostly, grammatical and/or logical form). Making these notions clear is notoriously hard; but the relevant intuitions are easy enough to grasp.

Whether John's utterance of "Mary might do it, but Joan is above that sort of thing" is ironical, say, is a question that can't be answered short of using a lot of what you know about John, Mary, and Joan. Worse yet, there doesn't seem to be any way to say, in the general case, how much, or precisely what, of what you know about them might need to be accessed in making such determinations. *Maybe* an interestingly encapsulated system could reliably recognize the irony (sincerity, metaphoricalness, rhetoricalness, etc.) of utterances, but there are certainly no plausible proposals about how this might be so. It looks as though recognizing such properties of utterances is typically an exercise in "inference to the best explanation": given what I know about John, and about what John thinks about Mary and Joan, he *couldn't* have meant that literally . . . etc. These are, of course, precisely the sorts of inferences that you would *not* expect encapsulated systems to perform. The "best" explanation is the one you want to accept *all things considered*, and encapsulated systems are prohibited by definition from considering all things.

Compare the computational problems involved in the recognition of linguistic form. The idea here is that the grammatical and logical structure of an utterance is uniquely determined (or, more precisely, uniquely determined up to ambiguity) by its phonetic constituency; and its phonetic constituency is uniquely determined in turn by certain of its acoustic properties (mutatis mutandis, the linguistic properties of written tokens are uniquely determined by certain properties of their shapes). "Acoustic" properties, according to this usage, are ipso facto transducer-detectable; so an input system that has access to the appropriate transduced representations of an utterance knows everything about the utterance that it needs to know to determine which sentential type it is a token of and, probably, what the logical form of the utterance is.[28] In short, if you are looking for an interesting property of utterances that might be computed by rigidly encapsulated systems—indeed, a property that might even be computed by largely bottom-to-top processors— then the type-identity of the utterance, together, perhaps, with its logical form would seem to be a natural candidate.

It is thus worth stressing that type-identity and at least some aspects of logical form are phenomenologically salient and are patently recognized 'on line'; moreover, the computation of type-identity is clearly an essential part of the overall process of language comprehension. In the general case, you can't understand what the speaker has said unless you can at least figure out which sentence he has uttered.

Is there, then, an encapsulated analyzer for logical and grammatical form? All the arguments are indirect; but, for what it's worth, it's rather hard to see how some of the processes that recognize logical and grammatical form could be anything but encapsulated. Background information can be brought to bear in perceptual analysis only where the property that is recognized is, to some significant extent, redundant in the context of recognition. But, as we remarked above, there doesn't seem to be much redundancy between context variables and the *form* of an utterance, however much context may predict its *content*. Even if you know precisely what someone is going to say—in the sense of knowing precisely which proposition he is going to assert—the knowledge buys you very little in predicting the type/token relation for his utterance; there are simply too many linguistically different ways of saying the same thing.

It is not, therefore, surprising that the more extreme proposals for context-driven language recognizers do *not* generally proceed by using contextual information to identify grammatical relations. Instead, they proceed whenever possible directly from a lexical analysis to a "conceptual" analysis—one which, in effect, collapses across synonymous tokens regardless of their linguistic type. It is unclear to me whether such models are proposed as serious candidates for the explanation of human communicative capacities, though sometimes I fear that they may be. (See, e.g., Schank and Abelson, 1975; for experimental evidence that linguistic form continues to have its effect as semantic integration increases, precisely as one would expect if the recovery of logical syntactic form is mandatory, see Forster and Olberi, 1973.) To put the point in a nutshell: linguistic form recognition can't be context-driven because context doesn't determine form; if linguistic form is recognized at all, it must be by largely encapsulated processes.

So the present proposal is that the language-input system specifies, for any utterance in its domain, its linguistic and maybe its logical form. It is implicit in this proposal that it does no more than that[29]—e.g., that it doesn't recover speech-act potential (except, perhaps, insofar as speech-act potential may be correlated with properties of form, as in English interrogative word order). As I suggested, the main argument for this proposal is that, on the one hand, type/token relations surely must be computed in the course of sentence comprehension and, on the other, it is hard to see how anything much richer than type/token relations could be computed by an informationally encapsulated processor. All this comports with the strong intuition that while there could perhaps be an algorithm for parsing, there surely could not be an algorithm for estimating communicative intentions in anything like their full diversity. Arguments about what an author *meant* are thus able to be interminable in ways in which arguments about what he *said* are not.

This is all pretty loose. Most dicussions in linguistics and psy-cholinguistics have been primarily interested in establishing *minimal* conditions on the output of the sentence processor, e.g., by dem-onstrating that one or another level of linguistic representation is "psychologically real" and recovered on line. By contrast, the prob-lem that arises in discussions of modularity is typically of the form: What is the *most* that an encapsulated processor should be supposed to compute? Which aspects of the input can plausibly be recognized without generalized appeal to background data? There is, however, one area of language research in which issues of this latter sort have been extensively discussed. It may be worth a brief recapi-tulation here, since it provides quite a clear illustration of what problems about determining the level of the perception/cognition interface are like.

Consider again the question of the vocabulary of an utterance (as opposed to its logicosyntactic form on the one hand and its propositional content on the other). Since I have assumed that input-processing yields type identifications, I am committed to the claim that the language processor delivers, for each input utterance, a representation which specifies its lexical constituents inter alia. (Utterances which differ in their lexical constituents are, of course, ipso facto distinct in type.) The present question is whether it is plausible to suppose that the language-input system provides still deeper representations at the lexical level.

A view that has been influential in both linguistics and psychology suggests that it does. According to this view, understanding an utterance involves recovering the *definitions* of such definable lexical items as it may contain. So, for example, understanding a token of "John is a bachelor" involves representing the utterance as con-taining a word that means *unmarried man*. Note that this is a claim about processes of *comprehension* and not, e.g., about inferential operations which may be applied to the internal representation of the utterance *after* it has been understood. It is thus natural to interpret the claim as implying that the recovery of definitions of lexical items takes place during input processing (viz., *interior* to the putative language module). We would thus expect, if the claim is true, that the recovery of definitional information should exhibit the typical properties of input processes: it should happen fast, it should be mandatory (insensitive to task demands), etc.

The alternative view is that the "surface" vocabulary of an utterance is preserved at the level of representation where the language processor interfaces with cognitive processes at large. There should thus be no level of analysis specified by the language-input system at which ". . . bachelor . . ." and ". . . unmarried man . . ." receive identical representations (though, of course, *post*comprehension inferential processes may indeed identify them as synonymous. One could imagine that such postcomprehension inferences might be mediated by the application of "meaning postulates" in something like the sense of Carnap (1960); for discussion, see Kintsch (1974), Fodor, Fodor and Garrett (1975).)

The currently available experimental evidence supports the latter view. (See Fodor et al., 1980.) In fact, so far as I know, there have been *no* convincing data in favor of the claim that representations of definitional content engage *any* sentence-comprehension process. The importance of imposing appropriate task demands in experimental tests of this claim can, however, hardly be overemphasized. There is, e.g., no doubt at all that definitionally related sentences tend to be conflated in experiments that require not just comprehension but recall as well. This is quite consonant with the view that memory is an inferential process par excellence (see Bartlett, 1932).

If these observations are correct, they strongly suggest that input-processing for language provides no semantic analysis "inside" lexical items. Or, to put it another way, the functionally defined level *output of the language processing module* respects such *structurally* defined notions as *item in the morphemic inventory of the language*. It is of primary importance to see that there is no a priori reason why this should be true.[30] That is, there is no a priori reason why the representations of utterances that are computed by fast, mandatory, informationally encapsulated, etc., etc., processes should constitute a representational level by *any* independent criteria. But, in the case of language at least, there is some a posteriori reason to believe that they do: on the one hand, there is strong evidence that such notions as *morphemic level* and *syntactic level* pick out coherent classes of representations; and, on the other, there are at least reasonable grounds for supposing that it is representations at these sorts of levels that the input system delivers.

By the way, the (presumptive) fact that the representations which input systems recover constitute linguistic natural kinds is a strong argument that the concept *input process* itself picks out a natural kind. Suppose that the representations of utterances that are recovered by fast, informationally encapsulated, mandatory, etc. processes turned out to specify, e.g., the second phoneme of the third word of each utterance, the intonation contour of its last five syllables, and the definitions of all the words that it contains which begin with 'u'. Since this collection of properties has no theoretical interest whatever, we would be inclined to infer that there is, to that extent, nothing interesting about the class of psycholinguistic processes that are fast, mandatory, and informationally encapsulated. But, apparently, that is *not* the sort of thing that we find. What we find instead is that the fast, mandatory . . . etc. processes deliver representations of utterances which make perfectly good sense considered *as* representations of utterances; representations which specify, for example, morphemic constituency, syntactic structure, and logical form. This is just the sort of thing you would expect if the fast, mandatory . . . etc. processes form a system that is functionally relevant to language comprehension. In particular, it is just what you would expect if language comprehension is effected by the sort of system that I am calling a module.

If I am inclined to harp on these points, it is because the opposed view—that sentence-processing grades off insensibly into inference and the appreciation of context; into general cognition in short— is actually predominant in the field. (Especially on the West Coast, where gurus teach that the All is One.) Suffice it to say that the choice between these pictures is empirical—not a matter of taste— and that such evidence as is actually germane seems not unfavorable to the modularity view.

The preceding discussion provides a context for raising analogous issues about vision. If the modularity story is to be plausible here, the output of the visual processor must be reasonably shallow (it should not categorize visual stimuli in such terms as *proton trace*), and it must form a level of representation by some independent criterion—i.e., there should be interesting things to say about the output representations other than that they are, de facto, the kinds of representations that the visual processor puts out.

Moreover, various candidates that satisfy the shallowness test and the levels test must nevertheless be rejected on grounds of phenomenological inaccessibility.[31] I am thinking of such representations as Marr's 'primal', '2.5 D', and '3 D' sketch (Marr and Nishihara, 1978). Such representations are certainly shallow enough. Indeed, they would seem to be too shallow. If we accept them as defining visual processor outputs, we shall have to say that even object recognition is not, strictly speaking, a phenomenon of visual perception, since, at these levels of representation, only certain geometric properties of the stimulus are specified. But, surely, from the point of view of phenomenological accessibility, perception is above all the recognition of objects and events. Shallower systems of representation can therefore constitute only interlevels of input analysis. What, then, is its output?

One of the most interesting ideas in recent cognitive theorizing is that there is a level of 'basic' perceptual objects (or, to use a slightly less misleading terminology, of basic perceptual categories). This notion is explored extensively in Brown (1958) and in Rosch et al. (1976), but a quick presentation may make the point. Consider a category hierarchy like *poodle, dog, mammal, animal, physical object, thing*. Roughly, the following seems to be true of such sets of categories: they effect a taxonomy of objects at increasing levels of abstractness, such that a given entity may belong to any or all of them, and such that the potential extensions of the categories increase as you go up the hierarchy (there are, as it were, more possible dogs than possible poodles; more possible animals than possible dogs; and so forth). Moreover, this is an *implicational* hierarchy in the sense that it is somehow *necessary* that whatever satisfies a category at the *n*th level of abstraction must always satisfy every category at higher-than-*n* levels of abstraction. (I don't care, for present purposes [actually, I don't think I care at all] whether this necessity is analytic or even whether it is linguistic. Suffice it that it is no accident that every poodle is a dog.)

The idea of *basic* categories is that some of the levels of abstraction in such implicational hierarchies have peculiar psychological salience. Intuitively, salience clusters at the "middle" levels of abstraction (in the present case, *dog* rather than *poodle* or *thing*). There is, alas, no independent definition of "middle," and it is quite conceivable that intuitions about which levels are in the middle just *are* intuitions of relative salience. Still, the fact seems to be that the following cluster of psychological properties tend to converge on the same member (or members) of each implicational hierarchy; that is, whatever member(s) of a hierarchy has one of them is also quite likely to have the rest. A category that has them all is paradigmatically basic.

(a) The basic category of a hierarchy often turns out to correspond to the high-frequency item in vocabulary counts; "dog" is thus a higher-frequency lexical item than either "animal" or "poodle."

(b) The word for the basic category of a hierarchy tends to be learned earlier than words that express other levels in the hierarchy (Anglin, 1979).

(c) The basic category is often the least abstract member of its hierarchy that is monomorphemically lexicalized. Compare "Sheraton wing-back armchair"; "armchair"; *"chair"*; "furniture"; "artifact"; "physical object . . ." In some domains there is evidence that the monomorphemic lexicalization of the basic category is universal—for example, there are few or no languages that have a single word for what we would call "a washed-out pinkish red" while coding what we would call plain "red" polymorphemically. (See Berlin and Kay, 1969.) As with (a) and (b), it seems natural to interpret (c) as a linguistic reflex of the relative psychological salience of the basic category as compared with other members of its hierarchy.

(d) Basic categories are natural candidates for ostensive introduction. "Dog" is ostensively definable for a child who hasn't learned "poodle," but it is probably not possible to teach "poodle" ostensively to a child who hasn't got "dog"; and it probably is not possible to teach "animal" ostensively to a child who hasn't got at least some animal words at the same level as "dog." This becomes glaringly obvious if one thinks about the relative ostensive definability of, e.g., "pale red," "red," and "color." Once again, it seems plausible to connect the relative ostensive definability of a word with the relative psychological salience of the property that the word expresses. (For a discussion of the implications of the correlation between basicness and ostensive definability, see Fodor, 1981a, chap. 10.)

(e) Basic categorizations yield 'information peaks' in the following sense. Ask a subject to list all the properties that come to mind when he thinks of *animals*; then ask him to list all the properties that come to mind when he thinks of *dogs*; and then ask him to list all the properties that come to mind when he thinks of *poodles*. One finds that one gets quite a lot more properties for *dog* than for *animal*, whereas the properties listed for *poodles* include very few more than one got for *dog*.[32] (See Rosch, et al., 1976.) It seems that—in some sense that is admittedly not very clear—basic categorizations are the ones that encode the most information per unit judgment. Taken together with Paul Grice's "maxim of quantity" (be informative) and his "maxim of manner" (be succinct), this observation predicts the following bit of pragmatics:

(f) Basic categories are the natural ones to use for describing things, ceteris paribus. "Ceteris paribus" means something like 'assuming that there are no special task demands in play'. You say to me, 'What do you see out the window?; I reply, 'A lady walking a dog', (rather than, e.g., 'A lady walking an animal' on the one hand, or 'A lady walking a silver-grey, miniature, poodle bitch', on the other. The point to notice here is that, all things being equal, the first is the preferred level of description even where I may happen to know enough to provide the third.

I assume that these linguistic facts are surface reflections of a deeper psychological reality, to wit:

(g) Basic categorizations are phenomenologically *given*; they provide, as it were, the natural level for describing things *to oneself*. A glance out the window thus reveals: a lady walking a *dog*, rather than a lady walking a silver-grey, miniature. . . etc. (Of course, sustained inspection alters all this. But phenomenological salience is accessibility *without* sustained inspection.) You might predict from these intuitions that perceptual identifications which involve the application of basic categories ought to be fast as compared to applications of either more or less abstract members of their implication hierarchies. There is, in fact, experimental evidence that this is true. (See Intraub, 1981.)

(h) Basic categories are typically the most abstract members of their implication hierarchies which subtend individuals of approximately similar appearance (Rosch, et al., 1976). So, roughly, you can draw something that is just a dog, but you can't draw something that is just an animal; you can draw something that is just a chair, but you can't draw something that is just furniture.

This observation suggests that, to a first approximation, basic categorizations (unlike categorizations that are more abstract) can be made, with reasonable reliability, on the basis of the visual properties of objects. It thus returns us to the issue of perception. Since input systems are, by assumption, informationally encapsulated (no generalized top-down access to background information), the categorizations such systems effect must be comprehensively determined by properties that the visual transducers can detect: shape, color, local motion, or whatever. Input systems aren't, of course, confined to encoding properties like shape and color, but they *are* confined—in virtue of their informational encapsulation—to categorizations which can be inferred, with reasonable accuracy, from such "purely visual" properties of the stimulus.[33] (Compare: the language processor is confined to recovering properties of the input token that can be inferred, with reasonable accuracy, from its acoustic properties—hence to recovering linguistic form rather than, say, the speaker's metaphorical intent.)

Putting it all together, then: basic categorizations are typically the most abstract members of their inferential hierarchies that *could* be assigned by an informationally encapsulated visual-input analyzer; more abstract categorizations are not reliably predicted by *visual* properties of the distal stimulus. And basic categorizations are the ones that you would want the input systems to deliver assuming that you are interested in maximizing the information per unit of perceptual integration (as, presumably, you are). So, the suggestion is that the visual-input system delivers basic categorizations.[34]

A lot follows from this suggestion: for example, that in one useful sense of the observation/theory distinction, dogs but not protons count as observed; that the outputs of the visual processor—like the outputs of the language processor—constitute a level of representation on grounds independent of the fact that they happen to be the set of representations that some input system delivers; that it is no accident that the phenomenologically accessible categorizations are expressed by ostensively definable words. And so forth. I leave it to the reader to draw the morals. Suffice it that the notion that visual analyses are computed by an informationally encapsulated system leads to the prediction that there should be some set of representations which are (roughly) shape-assignable on the one hand, and which, on the other hand, play a specially central role in the mental life of the organism. The pregnancy of the basic category construct suggests that this prediction is true.

III.7. Input systems are associated with
fixed neural architecture

Martin Gardner has a brief discussion of Gall in his *In the Name of Science* (1952). Gardner remarks that "Modern research on the brain has, as most everyone knows, completely demolished the old 'faculty psychology'. Only sensory centers are localized" (p. 293). The argument moves breathtakingly fast. Is faculty psychology literally incompatible with, say, an equipotential brain? Remember that faculties are, in the first instance, functionally rather than physiologically individuated. And perhaps *localization* isn't precisely the notion that Gardner wants, since, after all, there might be neural specificity of some functions that aren't localized in the sense of being associated with large, morphologically characterizable brain regions. Still, if you read "perceptual" for "sensory", and if you add language, and if you don't worry about the localization of motor and other noncognitive functions, there is something to what Gardner says. In particular, it seems that there is characteristic neural architecture associated with each of what I have been calling the input systems. Indeed, the following, stronger, claim seems to be approximately true: *all* the cases of massive neural structuring to which a content-specific cognitive function can confidently be assigned appear to be associated with input analysis, either with language or with perception. There is, to put it crudely, no known brain center for *modus ponens*.

I shall return presently to consider the implications of this observation. Suffice it, for the moment, that the intimate association of modular systems with neural hardwiring is pretty much what you would expect given the assumption that the key to modularity is informational encapsulation. Presumably, hardwired connections indicate privileged paths of informational access; the effect of hardwiring is thus to facilitate the flow of information from one neural structure to another. But, of course, what counts as relative *facilitation* when viewed one way counts as relative *encapsulation* when viewed the other way. If you facilitate the flow of information from A to B by hardwiring a connection between them, then you provide B with a kind of access to A that it doesn't have to locations C, D, E, . . . This sort of differential accessibility makes sense for a system only under the condition that it wants faster (easier, more continuous, anyhow cheaper) access to A than it does to C, D, E, and the rest. That is, it makes sense only for a system whose informational demands are relatively skewed. There is, in particular, no point in hardwiring the connections of paradigmatic *un*encapsulated systems—ones whose informational demands may be imposed anywhere at any time. Neural architecture, I'm suggesting, is the natural concomitant of informational encapsulation.

Anyhow, we do find neurological structure associated with the perceptual systems and with language. Whatever the right interpretation of this finding may be, it provides yet another reason to believe that the input systems constitute a natural kind.

III.8. Input systems exhibit characteristic and specific breakdown patterns

The existence of—and analogies between—relatively well defined pathological syndromes in the perceptual systems on the one hand and the language-processing mechanisms on the other has been too frequently noted to require much discussion here. There seems to be general agreement that the agnosias and aphasias constitute patterned failures of functioning—i.e., they cannot be explained by mere quantitative decrements in global, horizontal capacities like memory, attention, or problem-solving. This is hardly surprising if, on the one hand, input analysis is largely effected by specific, hardwired neural circuitry and, on the other, the pathologies of the input systems are caused by insult to these specialized circuits.

Contrast the central processes, which do not appear to be intimately associated with specific neural architecture and also do not appear to be prone to well defined breakdown syndromes. (It used to be thought that schizophrenia is a "pathology of thought," but I gather this view is no longer very popular.)

I don't, however, wish to overplay this point. Any psychological mechanism which is functionally distinct may presumably be selectively impaired, horizontal faculties included. There may thus quite possibly be pathologies of, say, memory or attention that are not domain specific in the way that the aphasias and agnosias are supposed to be; see, e.g., Milner, Corbin, and Teuber (1968). If so, then that is evidence (*contra* Gall) that such capacities are mediated by bona fide faculties and that they are horizontally organized. As previously remarked, the possibility of advancing mixed models in this area ought not to be ignored.

III.9.   The ontogeny of input systems exhibits a characteristic pace and sequencing

The issues here are so very moot, and the available information is so fragmentary, that I offer this point more as a hypothesis than a datum. There are, however, straws in the wind. There is now a considerable body of findings about the ontogenetic sequencing of language acquisition, and there are some data on the very early visual capacities of infants. These results are compatible, so far, with the view that a great deal of the developmental course of the input systems is endogenously determined. On the one hand, the capacity of infants for visual categorization appears to have been very seriously underestimated by empiricist theorizing (see the recent work of Spelke, 1982; Meltzoff, 1979; Bower, 1974; and others). And, on the other hand, linguistic performance—though obviously not present in the neonate—appears to develop in an orderly way that is highly sensitive to the maturational state of the organism, and surprisingly insensitive to deprivation of environmental information. (Goldin-Meadow and Feldman, 1977; Gleitman, 1981.) Moreover, language development appears to respect many of the universals of adult grammatical organization even at quite early stages (see Brown, 1973, and, papers in Takavolian, 1981). There have been occasional attempts to account for such apparently domain-specific features of ontogeny by appeal to the developing structure of 'problem-solving heuristics' or of 'general intelligence;' but they have been half-hearted and, in my view, quite unsuccessful when contemplated in detail. (For extensive discussion of these issues, see Piatelli-Palmarini, 1980, and the reviews by Marshall, 1981, and by Pylyshyn, 1981.) For what it's worth, then, no facts now available contradict the claim that the neural mechanisms subserving input analysis develop according to specific, endogenously determined patterns under the impact of environmental releasers. This picture is, of course, quite compatible with the view that these mechanisms are instantiated in correspondingly specific, hardwired neural structures. It is also compatible with the suggestion that much of the information at the disposal of such systems is innately specified; as, indeed, vertical faculty theorists from Gall to Chomsky have been wont to claim.

I have been arguing that the psychological systems whose operations "present the world to thought" constitute a natural kind by criteria independent of their similarity of function; there appears to be a cluster of properties that they have in common but which, *qua* input analyzers, they might perfectly well not have shared.[35] We can abbreviate all this by the claim that the input systems constitute a family of modules: domain-specific computational systems characterized by informational encapsulation, high-speed, restricted access, neural specificity, and the rest.

Let's suppose, probably contrary to fact, that you have found this story convincing. So, you are pretending to believe, for purposes of the following discussion, that the input systems are modular. If you actually did believe this, you would surely be led to pose the following question: are cognitive mechanisms *other than* input systems also modular? Or are the properties of being modular and being an input system coextensive? We are thus, finally, about to raise what I regard as the main issue: whether modularity is (as Gall, for example, thought it was) the *general* fact about the organization of the mind. I am going to suggest that at least some cognitive systems are nonmodular, and then I'm going to explore a variety of consequences of their (putative) nonmodularity.

PART IV

CENTRAL SYSTEMS

Vertical faculties are domain specific (by definition) and modular (by hypothesis). So the questions we now want to ask can be put like this: Are there psychological processes that can plausibly be assumed to cut across cognitive domains? And, if there are, is there reason to suppose that such processes are subserved by nonmodular (e.g., informationally unencapsulated) mechanisms?

The answer to the first of these questions is, I suppose, reasonably clear. Even if input systems are domain specific, there must be some cognitive mechanisms that are not. The general form of the argument goes back at least to Aristotle: the representations that input systems deliver have to interface somewhere, and the computational mechanisms that effect the interface must ipso facto have access to information from more than one cognitive domain. Consider:

(a) We have repeatedly distinguished between what the input systems compute and what the organism (consciously or subdoxastically) *believes*. Part of the point of this distinction is that input systems, being informationally encapsulated, typically compute representations of the distal layout on the basis of less information about the distal layout than the organism has available. Such representations want correction in light of background knowledge (e.g., information in memory) and of the simultaneous results of input analysis in other domains (see Aristotle on the 'common sense'). Call the process of arriving at such corrected representations "the fixation of perceptual belief." To a first approximation, we can assume that the mechanisms that effect this process work like this: they look simultaneously at the representations delivered by the various input systems and at the information currently in memory, and they arrive at a best (i.e., best available) hypothesis about how the world must be, given these various sorts of data.[36] But if there are mechanisms that fix perceptual belief, and if they work in anything like this way, then these mechanisms are not domain specific. Indeed, the point of having them is precisely to ensure that, wherever possible, what the organism believes is determined by all the information it has access to, regardless of which cognitive domains this information is drawn from.

(b) We use language (inter alia) to communicate our views on how the world is. But this use of language is possible only if the mechanisms that mediate the production of speech have access to what we see (or hear, or remember, or think) that the world is like. Since, by assumption, such mechanisms effect an interface among vertical faculties, they cannot themselves be domain specific. More precisely, they must at least be *less* domain specific than the vertical faculties are.[37]

(c) One aspect of the 'impenetrability' of the input systems is, we assumed, their insensitivity to the utilities of the organism. This assumption was required in part to explain the *veridicality* of perception given that the world doesn't always prove to be the way that we would prefer it to be. However, an interface between perception and utilities must take place *somewhere* if we are to use the information that input systems deliver in order to determine how we ought to act. (Decision theories are, to all intents and purposes, models of the structure of this interface. The point is, roughly, that wishful seeing is avoided by requiring interactions with utilities to occur *after*—not *during*—perceptual integration.) So, again, the moral seems to be that there must be some mechanisms which cross the domains that input systems establish.

For these and other similar reasons, I assume that there must be relatively nondenominational (i.e., domain-*in*specific) psychological systems which operate, inter alia, to exploit the information that input systems provide. Following the tradition, I shall call these "central" systems, and I will assume that it is the operation of these sorts of systems that people have in mind when they talk, pretheoretically, of such mental processes as thought and problem-solving. Central systems may be domain specific in *some* sense— we will consider this when we get to the issues about 'epistemic boundedness'—but at least they aren't domain specific in the way that input systems are. The interesting question about the central systems is whether, being nondenominational, they are also non-modular in other respects as well. That is, whether the central systems fail to exhibit the galaxy of properties that lead us to think of the input systems as a natural kind—the properties enumerated in Part III.

Briefly, my argument is going to be this: we have seen that much of what is typical of the input systems is more or less directly a product of their informational encapsulation. By contrast, I'll claim that central systems are, in important respects, *un*encapsulated, and that it is primarily for this reason that they are not plausibly viewed as modular. Notice that I am not going to be arguing for a tautology. It is perfectly possible, in point of logic, that a system which is *not* domain specific might nevertheless be encapsulated. Roughly, domain specificity has to do with the range of questions for which a device provides answers (the range of inputs for which it computes analyses); whereas encapsulation has to do with the range of information that the device consults in deciding what answers to provide. A system could thus be domain specific but unencapsulated (it answers a relatively narrow range of questions but in doing so it uses whatever it knows); and a system could be nondenominational but encapsulated (it will give some answer to any question; but it gives its answers off the top of its head—i.e., by reference to less than all the relevant information). If, in short, it is true that only domain-specific systems are encapsulated, then that truth is interesting. Perhaps it goes without saying that I am not about to demonstrate this putative truth. I am, however, about to explore it.

So much for what I'm going to be arguing *for*. Now a little about the strategy of the argument. The fact is that there is practically no direct evidence, pro or con, on the question whether central systems are modular. No doubt it is possible to achieve some gross factoring of "intelligence' into "verbal" versus "mathematical/spatial" capacities; and no doubt there is something to the idea of a corresponding hemispheric specialization. But such dichotomies are *very* gross and may themselves be confounded with the modularity of the input systems—that is to say, they give very little evidence for the existence of domain-specific (to say nothing of modular) systems other than the ones that subserve the functions of perceptual and linguistic analysis.

When you run out of direct evidence, you might just as well try arguing from analogies, and that is what I propose to do. I have been assuming that the typical function of central systems is the fixation of belief (perceptual or otherwise) by nondemonstrative inference. Central systems look at what the input systems deliver, and they look at what is in memory, and they use this information to constrain the computation of 'best hypotheses' about what the world is like. These processes are, of course, largely unconscious, and very little is known about their operation. However, it seems reasonable enough that something can be inferred about them from what we know about *explicit* processes of nondemonstrative inference—viz., from what we know about empirical inference in science. So, here is how I am going to proceed. First, I'll suggest that scientific confirmation—the nondemonstrative fixation of belief in science—is typically unencapsulated. I'll then argue that if, pursuing the analogy, we assume that the central psychological systems are also unencapsulated, we get a picture of those systems that is, anyhow, not radically implausible given such information about them as is currently available.

The nondemonstrative fixation of belief in science has two properties which, though widely acknowledged, have not (so far as I know) yet been named. I shall name them: confirmation in science is *isotropic* and it is *Quineian*. It is notoriously hard to give anything approaching a rigorous account of what being isotropic and Quineian amounts to, but it is easy enough to convey the intuitions.

By saying that confirmation is isotropic, I mean that the facts relevant to the confirmation of a scientific hypothesis may be drawn from anywhere in the field of previously established empirical (or, of course, demonstrative) truths. Crudely: everything that the scientist knows is, in principle, relevant to determining what else he ought to believe. In principle, our botany constrains our astronomy, if only we could think of ways to make them connect.

As is usual in a methodological inquiry, it is possible to consider the isotropy of confirmation either normatively (as a principle to which we believe that rational inductive practice *ought* to conform) or sociologically (as a principle which working scientists actually adhere to in assessing the degree of confirmation of their theories). In neither case, however, should we view the isotropy of confirmation as merely gratuitous—or, to use a term of Rorty's (1979) as merely "optional." If isotropic confirmation 'partially defines the language game that scientists play' (remember when we used to talk that way?), that is because of a profound conviction—partly metaphysical and partly epistemological—to which scientists implicitly subscribe: the world is a connected causal system *and we don't know how the connections are arranged.* Because we don't, we must be prepared to abandon previous estimates of confirmational relevance as our scientific theories change. The points of all this is: confirmational isotropy is a reasonable property for nondemonstrative inference to have because the goal of nondemonstrative inference is to determine the truth about a causal mechanism—the world—of whose workings we are arbitrarily ignorant. That is why our institution of scientific confirmation is isotropic, and it is why it is plausible to suppose that what psychologists call "problem-solving" (i.e., nondemonstrative inference in the service of individual fixation of belief) is probably isotropic too.

The isotropy of scientific confirmation has sometimes been denied, but never, I think, very convincingly. For example, according to some historians it was part of the Aristotelian strategy against Galileo to claim that no data other than observations of the movements of astronomical objects could, in principle, be relevant to the (dis)confirmation of the geocentric theory. Telescopic observations of the phases of Venus were thus ruled irrelevant a priori. In notably similar spirit, some linguists have recently claimed that no data except certain specified kinds of facts about the intuitions of native speakers could, in principle, be relevant to the (dis)confirmation of grammatical theories. Experimental observations from psycholinguistics are thus ruled irrelevant a priori. However, this sort of methodology seems a lot like special pleading: you tend to get it precisely when cherished theories are in trouble from prima facie disconfirming data. Moreover, it often comports with Conventionalist construals of the theories so defended. That is, theories for which nonisotropic confirmation is claimed are often viewed, even by their proponents, as merely mechanisms for making predictions; what is alleged in their favor is predictive adequacy rather than correspondence to the world. (Viewed from our perspective, nonisotropic confirmation is, to that extent, not a procedure for fixation of belief, since, on the Conventionalist construal, the predictive adequacy of a theory is *not* a reason for believing that the theory is *true*.)

One final thought on the isotropy issue. We are interested in isotropic systems because such systems are ipso facto unencapsulated. We are interested in scientific confirmation because (a) there is every reason to suppose that it is isotropic; (b) there is every reason to suppose that it is a process fundamentally similar to the fixation of belief; and (c) it is perhaps the only "global", unencapsulated, wholistic cognitive process about which anything is known that's worth reporting. For all that, scientific *confirmation* is probably not the best place to look if you want to see cognitive isotropy writ large. The best place to look, at least if one is willing to trust the anecdotes, is scientific *discovery*.

What the anecdotes say about scientific discovery—and they say it with a considerable show of univocality (see, e.g., papers in Ortony, 1979)—is that some sort of 'analogical reasoning' often plays a central role. It seems to me that we are thoroughly in the dark here, so I don't propose to push this point very hard. But it really does look as though there have been frequent examples in the history of science where the structure of theories in a new subject area has been borrowed from, or at least suggested by, theories *in situ* in some quite different domain: what's known about the flow of water gets borrowed to model the flow of electricity; what's known about the structure of the solar system gets borrowed to model the structure of the atom; what's known about the behavior of the market gets borrowed to model the process of natural selection, which in turn gets borrowed to model the shaping of operant responses. And so forth. The point about all this is that "analogical reasoning" would seem to be isotropy in the purest form: a process which depends precisely upon the transfer of information among cognitive domains previously assumed to be mutually irrelevant. By definition, encapsulated systems do not reason analogically.

I want to suggest two morals before I leave this point. The first is that the closer we get to what we are pretheoretically inclined to think of as the 'higher,' 'more intelligent', less reflexive, less routine exercises of cognitive capacities, the more such global properties as isotropy tend to show up. I doubt that this is an accident. I suspect that it is precisely its possession of such global properties that we have in mind when we think of a cognitive process as paradigmatically intelligent. The second moral preshadows a point that I shall jump up and down about further on. It is striking that, while everybody thinks that analogical reasoning is an important ingredient in all sorts of cognitive achievements that we prize, nobody knows anything about how it works; not even in the dim, in-a-glass-darkly sort of way in which there are some ideas about how confirmation works. I don't think that this is an accident either. In fact, I should like to propose a generalization; one which I fondly hope will some day come to be known as 'Fodor's First Law of the Nonexistence of Cognitive Science'. It goes like this: the more global (e.g., the more isotropic) a cognitive process is, the less anybody understands it. *Very* global processes, like analogical reasoning, aren't understood at all. More about such matters in the last part of this discussion.

By saying that scientific confirmation is Quineian, I mean that the degree of confirmation assigned to any given hypothesis is sensitive to properties of the entire belief system; as it were, the shape of our whole science bears on the epistemic status of each scientific hypothesis. Notice that being Quineian and being isotropic are not the same properties, though they are intimately related. For example, if scientific confirmation is isotropic, it is quite possible that some fact about photosynthesis in algae should be relevant to the confirmation of some hypothesis in astrophics ("the universe in a grain of sand" and all that). But the point about being Quineian is that we might have two astrophysical theories, both of which make the same predictions about algae and about everything else that we can think of to test, but such that one of the theories is better confirmed than the other—e.g., on grounds of such considerations as simplicity, plausibility, or conservatism. The point is that simplicity, plausibility, and conservatism are properties that theories have in virtue of their relation to the whole structure of scientific beliefs *taken collectively*. A measure of conservatism or simplicity would be a metric over *global* properties of belief systems.

Consider, by way of a simple example, Goodman's original (1954) treatment of the notion of projectability. We know that two hypotheses that are equivalent in respect of all the available data may nevertheless differ in their level of confirmation depending on which is the more projectable. Now, according to Goodman's treatment, the projectability of a hypothesis is inherited (at least in part) from the projectability of its vocabulary, and the projectability of an item of scientific vocabulary is determined by the (weighted?) frequency with which that item *has been projected* in previously successful scientific theories. So, the whole history of past projections contributes to determining the projectability of any given hypothesis on Goodman's account, and the projectability of a hypothesis (partially) determines its level of confirmation. Similarly with such notions as simplicity, conservatism, and the rest if only we knew how to measure them.

The idea that scientific confirmation is Quineian is by no means untendentious. On the contrary, it was a legacy of traditional philosophy of science—one of the "dogmas of Empiricism" (Quine, 1953) that there must be *semantic* connections between each theory statement and some data statements. That is, each hypothesis about "unobservables" must *entail* some predictions about observables, such entailments holding in virtue of the meanings of the theoretical terms that the hypotheses contain.[38] The effect of postulating such connections would be to determine a priori that certain data would disconfirm certain hypotheses, *whatever the shape of the rest of one's science might be*. For, of course, if H entails O, the discovery that –O would entail that –H. To that extent, the (dis)confirmation of

H by –O is independent of global features of the belief system that H and O belong to. To postulate meaning relations between data statements and theory statements is thus to treat confirmation as a *local* phenomenon rather than a global one.

I emphasize this consideration because analogous semantic proposals can readily be found in the psychological literature. For example, in the sorts of cognitive theories espoused by, say, Bruner or Vygotsky (and, more recently, in the work of the "procedural" semanticists), it is taken for granted that there must be connections of meaning between 'concepts' and 'percepts'. Basically, according to such theories, concepts are recipes for sorting stimuli into categories. Each recipe specifies a (more or less determinate) galaxy of tests that one can perform to effect a sorting, and each stimulus category is identified with a (more or less determinate) set of outcomes of the tests. To put the idea crudely but near enough for present purposes, there's a rule that you can test for *dog* by finding out if a thing barks, and the claim is that this rule is constitutive (though not, of course, exhaustive) of the concept *dog*. Since it is alleged to be a *conceptual* truth that whether it barks is relevant to whether it's a dog, it follows that the confirmation relation between "a thing is a dog" and "it barks" is insensitive to global properties of one's belief system. So considerations of theoretical simplicity etc. *could* not, even in principle, lead to the conclusion that whether it barks is *ir*relevant to whether it's a dog. To embrace that conclusion would be to change the concept.

This sort of example makes it clear how closely related being Quineian and being isotropic are. Since, on the view just scouted, it is a matter of *meaning* that barking is relevant to dogness, it is not possible to discover on empirical grounds that one was wrong about that relevancy relation. But isotropy is the principle that *any* fact may turn out to be (ir)relevant to the confirmation of any other. The Bruner-Vygotsky-procedural semantics line is thus incompatible with the isotropy of confirmation as well as with its Quineianness.

In saying that confirmation is isotropic and Quineian, I am thus consciously disgreeing with major traditions in the philosophy of science and in cognitive psychology. Nevertheless, I shall take it for granted that scientific confirmation is Quineian and isotropic. (Those who wish to see the arguments should refer to such classic papers in the modern philosophy of science as Quine, 1953, and

Putnam, 1962.) Moreover, since I am committed to relying upon the analogy between scientific confirmation and psychological fixation of belief, I shall take it for granted that the latter must be Quineian and isotropic too, hence that the Bruner-Vygotsky-procedural semantics tradition in cognitive psychology must be mistaken. I propose, at this point, to be both explicit and emphatic. The argument is that the central processes which mediate the fixation of belief are typically processes of rational nondemonstrative inference and that, since processes of rational nondemonstrative inference are Quineian and isotropic, so too are central processes. In particular, the theory of such processes must be consonant with the principle that the level of acceptance of any belief is sensitive to the level of acceptance of any other and to global properties of the field of beliefs taken collectively.

Given these assumptions, I have now got two things to do: I need to show that this picture of the central processes is broadly incompatible with the assumption that they are modular, and I need to show that it is a picture that has some plausibility independent of the putative analogy between cognitive psychology and the philosophy of science.

I take it that the first of these claims is relatively uncontroversial. We argued that modularity is fundamentally a matter of informational encapsulation and, of course, informationally encapsulated is precisely what Quineian/isotropic systems are not. When we discussed input systems, we thought of them as mechanisms for projecting and confirming hypotheses. And we remarked that, viewed that way, the informational encapsulation of such systems is tantamount to a constraint on the confirmation metrics that they employ; the confirmation metric of an encapsulated system is allowed to 'look at' only a certain restricted class of data in determining which hypothesis to accept. If, in particular, the flow of information through such a system is literally bottom-to-top, then its informational encapsulation consists in the fact that the ith-level hypotheses are (dis)confirmed solely by reference to lower-than-ith level representations. And even if the flow of data is unconstrained *within* a module, encapsulation implies constraints upon the access of intramodular processes to extramodular information sources. Whereas, by contrast, isotropy is by definition the property that a system has when it can look at anything it knows about in the course of determining the confirmation levels of hypotheses. So, in general, the more isotropic a confirmation metric is, the more heterogeneous the provenance of the data that it accepts as relevant to constraining its decisions. Scientific confirmation is isotropic in the limit in this respect; it provides a model of what the *non*modular fixation of belief is like.

Similarly with being Quineian. Quineian confirmation metrics are ipso facto sensitive to global properties of belief systems. Now, an informationally encapsulated system *could*, strictly speaking, nevertheless be Quineian. Simplicity, for example, could constrain confirmation even in a system which computes its simplicity scores over some arbitrarily selected subset of beliefs. But this is mere niggling about the letter. In spirit, global criteria for the evaluation of hypotheses comport most naturally with isotropic principles for the relevance of evidence. Indeed, it is only on the assumption that the selection of evidence is isotropic that considerations of simplicity (and other such global properties of hypotheses) are *rational* determinants of belief. It is epistemically interesting that H & T is a simpler theory than -H & T where H is a hypothesis to be evaluated and T is the rest of what one believes. But there is no interest in the analogous consideration where T is some *arbitrarily delimited* subset of one's beliefs. Where relevance is non-isotropic, assessments of relative simplicity can be gerrymandered to favor any hypothesis one likes. This is one of the reasons why the operation of (by assumption informationally encapsulated) input systems should not be identified with the fixation of perceptual belief; not, at least, by those who wish to view the fixation of perceptual belief as by and large a rational process.

So it seems clear that isotropic/Quineian systems are ipso facto unencapsulated; and if unencapsulated, then presumably non-modular. Or rather, since this is all a matter of degree, we had best say that *to the extent that* a system is Quineian and isotropic, it is also nonmodular. If, in short, isotropic and Quineian considerations are especially pressing in determining the course of the computations that central systems perform, it should follow that these systems differ in their computational character from the vertical faculties.

We are coming close to what we started out to find: an overall taxonomy of cognitive systems. According to the present proposal, there are, at a minimum, two families of such systems: modules (which are, relatively, domain specific and encapsulated) and central processes (which are, relatively, domain neutral and isotropic/Quineian). We have suggested that the characteristic function of modular cognitive systems is input analysis and that the characteristic function of central processes is the fixation of belief. If this is right, then we have three ways of taxonomizing cognitive processes which prove to be coextensive:

FUNCTIONAL TAXONOMY: input analysis versus fixation of belief
TAXONOMY BY SUBJECT MATTER: domain specific versus domain neutral
TAXONOMY BY COMPUTATIONAL CHARACTER: encapsulated versus Quineian/isotropic

I repeat that this coextension, if it holds at all, holds contingently. Nothing in point of logic stops one from imagining that these categories cross-classify the cognitive systems. If they do not, then that is a fact about the structure of the mind. Indeed, it is a *deep* fact about the structure of the mind.

All of which would be considerably more impressive if there were better evidence for the view of central processes that I have been proposing. Thus far, that account rests entirely on the analogy between psychological processes of belief fixation and a certain story about the character of scientific confirmation. There is very little that I can do about this, given the current underdeveloped state of psychological theories of thought and problem-solving. For what it's worth, however, I want to suggest two considerations that seem relevant and promising.

The first is that the difficulties we encounter when we try to construct theories of central processes are just the sort we would expect to encounter if such processes are, in essential respects, Quineian/isotropic rather than encapsulated. The crux in the construction of such theories is that there seems to be no way to delimit the sorts of informational resources which may affect, or be affected by, central processes of problem-solving. We can't, that is to say, plausibly view the fixation of belief as effected by computations over bounded, local information structures. A graphic example of this sort of difficulty arises in AI, where it has come to be known as the "frame problem" (i.e., the problem of putting a "frame" around the set of beliefs that may need to be revised in light of specified newly available information. Cf. the discussion in McCarthy and Hayes, 1969, from which the following example is drawn).

To see what's going on, suppose you were interested in constructing a robot capable of coping with routine tasks in familiar human environments. In particular, the robot is presented with the job of phoning Mary and finding out whether she will be late for dinner. Let's assume that the robot 'knows' it can get Mary's number by consulting the directory. So it looks up Mary's number and proceeds to dial. So far, so good. But now, notice that commencing to dial has all sorts of direct and indirect effects on the state of the world (including, of course, the internal state of the robot), and some of these effects are ones that the device needs to keep in mind for the guidance of its future actions and expectations. For example, when the dialing commences, the phone ceases to be free to outside calls; the robot's fingers (or whatever) undergo appropriate alterations of spatial location; the dial tone cuts off and gets replaced by beeps; something happens in a computer at Murray Hill; and so forth. Some (but, in principle, not all) such consequences are ones that the robot must be designed to monitor since they are relevant to "updating" beliefs upon which it may eventually come to act. Well, *which* consequences? The problem has at least the following components. The robot must be able to identify, with reasonable accuracy, those of its previous beliefs whose truth values may be expected to alter as a result of its current activities; and it must have access to systems that do whatever computing is involved in effecting the alterations.

Notice that, unless these circuits are arranged correctly, things can go absurdly wrong. Suppose that, having consulted the directory, the robot has determined that Mary's number is 222-2222, which number it commences to dial, pursuant to instructions previously received. But now it occurs to the machine that *one of the beliefs that may need updating in consequence of its having commenced dialing is its (recently acquired) belief about Mary's telephone number.* So, of course, it stops dialing and goes and looks up Mary's telephone number (again). Repeat, *da capo*, as many times as may amuse you. Clearly, we have here all the makings of a computational trap. Unless the robot can be assured that some of its beliefs are invariant under some of its actions, it will never get to *do* anything.

How, then, does the machine's program determine which beliefs the robot ought to reevaluate given that it has embarked upon some or other course of action? What makes this problem so hard is precisely that it seems unlikely that any *local* solution will do the job. For example, the following truths appear to be self-evident: First, that there is no fixed set of beliefs such that, for any action, those and only those beliefs are the ones that require reconsideration. (That is, which beliefs are up for grabs depends intimately upon which actions are performed and upon the context of the performances. There are *some*—indeed, indefinitely many—actions which, if performed, *should* lead one to consider the possibility that Mary's telephone number has changed in consequence.) Second, new beliefs don't come docketed with information about which old beliefs they ought to affect. On the contrary, we are forever being surprised by the implications of what we know, including, of course, what we know about the actions we perform. Third, the set of beliefs apt for reconsideration cannot be determined by reference to the recency of their acquisition, or by reference to their generality, or by reference to merely semantic relations between the contents of the beliefs and the description under which the action is performed . . . etc. Should any of these propositions seem *less* than self-evident, consider the special case of the frame problem where the robot is a mechanical scientist and the action performed is an experiment. Here the question 'which of my beliefs ought I to reconsider given the possible consequences of my action' is transparently equivalent to the question "What, in general, is the optimal adjustment of my beliefs to my experiences?" This is, of course, exactly the question that a theory of confirmation is supposed to answer; and, as we have been at pains to notice, confirmation is not a relation reconstructible by reference to local properties of hypotheses or of the data that bear upon them.

I am suggesting that, as soon as we begin to look at cognitive processes other than input analysis—in particular, at central processes of nondemonstrative fixation of belief—we run into problems that have a quite characteristic property. They seem to involve isotropic and Quineian computations; computations that are, in one or other respect, sensitive to the whole belief system. This is exactly what one would expect on the assumption that nondemonstrative fixation of belief really is quite like scientific confirmation, and that scientific confirmation is itself characteristically Quineian and iso-tropic. In this respect, it seems to me, the frame problem is par-adigmatic, and in this respect the seriousness of the frame problem has not been adequately appreciated.

For example, Raphael (1971) comments as follows: "(An intel-ligent robot) will have to be able to carry out tasks. Since a task generally involves some change in the world, it must be able to update its model (of the world) so it remains as accurate during and after the performance of a task as it was before. Moreover, it must be able to *plan* how to carry out a task, and this planning process usually requires keeping 'in mind' simultaneously a variety of possible actions and corresponding models of hypothetical worlds that would result from those actions. The bookkeeping problems involved with keeping track of these hypothetical worlds account for much of the difficulty of the frame problem" (p. 159). This makes it look as though the problem is primarily (a) how to notate the possible worlds and (b) how to keep track of the *demonstrative* consequences of changing state descriptions. But the deeper prob-lem, surely, is to keep track of the *non*demonstrative consequences. Slightly more precisely, the problem is, given an arbitrary belief world W and a new state description 'a is F', what is the appropriate successor belief world W'? What ought the device to believe, given that it used to believe W and now believes that a is F? But this isn't just a bookkeeping problem; it is the general problem of in-ductive confirmation.[39]

So far as I can tell, the usual assumption about the frame problem in AI is that it is somehow to be solved 'heuristically'. The idea is that, while nondemonstrative confirmation (and hence, presumably, the psychology of belief fixation) is isotropic and Quineian *in prin-ciple*, still, given a particular hypothesis, there are, in practice, heu-ristic procedures for determining the range of effects its acceptance can have on the rest of one's beliefs. Since these procedures are by assumption merely heuristic, they may be assumed to be local— i.e., to be sensitive to less than the whole of the belief systems to which they apply. Something like this may indeed be true; there is certainly considerable evidence for heuristic short-cutting in belief fixation, deriving both from studies of the psychology of problem-solving (for a recent review, see Nisbett and Ross, 1980) and from the sociology of science (Kuhn, 1970). In such cases, it is possible to show how potentially relevant considerations are often system-atically ignored, or distorted, or misconstrued in favor of relatively local (and, of course, highly fallible) problem-solving strategies. Perhaps a bundle of such heuristics, properly coordinated and rap-idly deployed, would suffice to make the central processes of a robot as Quinean and isotropic as yours, or mine, or the practicing scientist's ever actualy succeed in being. Since there are, at present, no serious proposals about what heuristics might belong to such a bundle, it seems hardly worth arguing the point.

Still, I am going to argue it a little.

There are those who hold that ideas recently evolved in AI—such notion as, e.g., those of 'frame' (see Minsky, 1975)[40] or 'script' (see Schank and Abelson, 1975)—will illuminate the problems about the globality of belief fixation since they do, in a certain sense, provide for placing a frame around the body of information that gets called when a given sort of problem is encountered. (For a discussion that runs along these optimistic lines, see Thagard, 1980.) It seems to me, however, that the appearance of progress here is entirely illusory—a prime case of confusing a notation with a theory.

If there were a principled solution to the frame problem, then no doubt that solution could be expressed as a constraint on the scripts, or frames, to which a given process of induction has access. But, lacking such a solution, there is simply no content to the idea that only the information represented in the frame (/script) that a problem elicits is computationally available for solving the problem. For one thing, since there are precisely no constraints on the in-dividuation of frames (/scripts), *any* two pieces of information can belong to the same frame (/script) at the discretion of the pro-grammer. This is just a way of saying that the solution of the frame problem can be accommodated to the frame (/script) notation *whatever that solution turns out to be*. Which is just another way of saying that the notation does not constrain the solution. Second, it is a widely advertised property of frames (/scripts) that they can cross-reference to one another. The frame for Socrates says, among other things, 'see Plato' . . . and so forth. There is no reason to doubt that, in any developed model, the system of cross-referencing would imply a graph in which there is a route (of greater or lesser length) from each point to any other. But now we have the frame problem all over again, in the form: Which such paths should actually be traversed in a given case of problem-solving, and what should bound the length of the trip? All that has happened is that, instead of thinking of the frame problem as an issue in the logic of confirmation, we are now invited to think of it as an issue in the theory of executive control (a change which there is, by the way, no reason to assume is for the better). More of this presently.

For now, let's summarize the major line of argument. If we assume that central processes are Quineian and isotropic, then we ought to predict that certain kinds of problems will emerge when we try to construct psychological theories which simulate such processes or otherwise explain them; specifically, we should predict problems that involve the characterization of nonlocal computational mechanisms. By contrast, such problems should not loom large for theories of psychological modules. Since, by assumption, modular systems are informationally encapsulated, it follows that the computations they perform are relatively local. It seems to me that these predictions are in reasonably good accord with the way that the problems of cognitive science have in fact matured: the input systems appear to be primarily stimulus driven, hence to exploit computational processes that are relatively insensitive to the general structure of the organism's belief system. Whereas, when we turn to the fixation of belief, we get a complex of problems that appear to be intractable precisely because they concern mental processes that aren't local. Of these, the frame problem is, as we have seen, a microcosm.

I have been marshaling considerations in favor of the view that central processes are Quineian/isotropic. That is what the analogy to scientific confirmation suggests that they ought to be, and the structure of the problems that arise in attempts to model central processes is quite compatible with that view of them. I now add that the view of central processes as computationally global can perhaps claim some degree of neurological plausibility. The picture of the brain that it suggests is a reasonably decent first approximation to the kind of brain that it appears we actually have.

When we discussed input analyzers, I commented on the natural connection between informational encapsulation and fixed neural architecture. Roughly, standing restrictions on information flow imply the option of hardwiring. If, in the extreme case, system B is required to take note of information from system A and is allowed to take note of information from nowhere else, you might as well build your brain with a permanent neuroanatomical connection from A to B. It is, in short, reasonable to expect biases in the distribution of information to mental processes to show up as structural biases in neural architecture.

Consider, by contrast, Quineian/isotropic systems, where more or less any subsystem may want to talk to any other at more or less any time. In this case, you'd expect the corresponding neuroanatomy to be relatively diffuse. At the limit, you might as well have a random net, with each computational subsystem connected, directly or indirectly, with every other; a kind of wiring in which you get a minimum of stable correspondence between neuroanatomical form and psychological function. The point is that in Quineian/isotropic systems, it may be *unstable, instantaneous* connectivity that counts. Instead of hardwiring, you get a connectivity that changes from moment to moment as dictated by the interaction between the program that is being executed and the structure of the task in hand. The moral would seem to be that computational isotropy comports naturally with neural isotropy (with what Lashley called "equipotentiality" of neural structure) in much the same way that informational encapsulation comports naturally with the elaboration of neural hardwiring.

So, if input analysis is modular and thought is Quineian/isotropic, you might expect a kind of brain in which there is stable neural architecture associated with perception-and-language but not with thought. And, I suggest, this seems to be pretty much what we in fact find. There is, as I remarked above, quite a lot that can be said about the neural specificity of the perceptual and linguistic mechanisms: at worst we can enumerate in some detail the parts of the brain that handle them; and at best we can exhibit characteristic neural architecture in the areas where these functions are performed. And then there are the rest of the higher brain systems (cf. what used to be called "association cortex"), in which neural connectivity appears to go every which way and the form/function correspondence appears to be minimal. There is some historical irony in all this. Gall argued from a (vertical) faculty psychology to the macroscopic differentiation of the brain. Flourens, his archantagonist, argued from the unity of the Cartesian ego to the brain's equipotentiality (see Bynum, op. cit.). The present suggestion is that they were *both* right.[41]

I am, heaven knows, not about to set up as an expert on neuropsychology, and I am painfully aware how impressionistic this all is. But while we're collecting impressions, I think the following one is striking. A recent issue of *Scientific American* (September, 1979) was devoted to the brain. Its table of contents is quite as interesting as the papers it contains. There are, as you might expect, articles that cover the neuropsychology of language and of the perceptual mechanisms. But there is nothing on the neuropsychology of thought—presumably because nothing is known about the neuropsychology of thought. I am suggesting that there is a good reason why nothing is known about it—namely, that there is nothing *to* know about it. You get form/function correspondence for the modular processes (specifically, for the input systems); but, in the case of central processes, you get an approximation to universal connectivity, hence no stable neural architecture to write *Scientific American* articles about.

To put these claims in a nutshell; there are *no* content-specific central processes for the performance of which correspondingly specific neural structures have been identified. Everything we now know is compatible with the claim that central problem-solving is subserved by equipotential neural mechanisms. This is precisely what you would expect if you assume that the central cognitive processes are largely Quineian and isotropic.

PART V
CAVEATS AND CONCLUSIONS

We now have before us what might be called a 'modified' modularity theory of cognitive processes. According to this theory, Gall was right in claiming that there are vertical faculties (domain specific computational mechanisms). Indeed, a still stronger claim is plausible: that the vertical faculties are modules (informationally encapsulated, neurologically hardwired, innately specified and so forth). But nonmodular cognitive systems are also acknowledged, and it is left open that these latter may exhibit features of horizontal organization. Roughly speaking, on this account, the distinction between vertical and horizontal modes of computational organization is taken to be coextensive with the functional distinction between systems of input analysis and systems that subserve the fixation of belief.

Given all of this, what I propose to do in the discussion that follows is to consider how this general view bears on some epistemological and methodological issues that have recently got tangled up with issues about modularity. And I want to make a couple of gloomy remarks about the implications of the modified modularity thesis for the practical prospects of cognitive science.

For purposes of the following discussion, let's forget that the modularity theory we have actually adopted is the modified one. Suppose, then, that Gall had been entirely right and the mind proved to be exhaustively a bundle of vertical faculties. Certain rather striking epistemological consequences would then seem to be entrained. Modular systems are, by definition *special purpose* computational mechanisms. If the mind is a collection of such mechanisms, then there are presumably going to be at least *some* purposes for which the mind *isn't fit*. Specifically, if each 'mental organ' is pretuned to the solution of computational problems with a specific sort of structure, then it is surely in the cards that there should be some problems whose structure the mind has no computational resources for coping with. Perhaps, indeed, there are some *important* problems of which this is true. For example, it is entirely compatible with a modularity theory that there should be endogenously determined constraints on our mental capacities such that the best science—the true theory of the structure of the world— is not one of the theories that we are capable of entertaining. Let us have a name for this thesis: I will say that a psychological theory represents the mind as *epistemically bounded* if it is a consequence of the theory that our cognitive organization imposes epistemically significant constraints on the beliefs that we can entertain.

The point of present interest is that the (plausible) claim that the modularity thesis implies epistemic boundedness has led to a certain amount of irrelevant criticism of the former doctrine. In particular, the way the discussion in the literature has gone has made it seem that the dispute between the modularity theory and its antagonists is a dispute between epistemic optimism and epistemic despair. The prevalent picture seems to be this: If the mind is modular, then, in all likelihood, we are epistemically bounded; whereas if, by contrast, God has endowed us with some form of *general* (hence nonmodular) intelligence, then there is perhaps no endogenously determined bound upon the class of truths that we can aspire to know. We may fail to find the true science for, as it were, exogenous reasons; because, for example, our spatiotemporal situation in the universe precludes access to the crucial data. But at least there is no enemy *within* the gates. If we don't succeed, that is not because we were built to fail.

This is very moving, but it is also quite beside the point. It is simply a mistake to suppose that if intelligence is general *in the sense of being nonmodular*, then it somehow follows (or even is somehow rendered plausible) that we are epistemically unbounded. In fact, I strongly suspect that the notion of epistemic unboundedness is just incoherent *whatever* view you take of the modularity issues (so long as one is assuming a Realist interpretation of science and a correspondence theory of truth). This all requires some discussion.

Let us retreat to the high ground where all systems that perform nondemonstrative inferences, modular or otherwise, fall together as hypothesis projecting/confirming devices. It was implicit in our earlier discussion that such a system must have access, at a minimum, to:

(a) A source of hypotheses to be (dis)confirmed.
(b) A data base
(c) A metric which can compute the confirmation level of a given hypothesis relative to a given data base.

Consider, now, how such a device might be so organized that it fails, in virtue of features of its organization, to pick the best hypothesis for the available data.

There are, to begin with, boring possibilities associated with parametric limitations of one sort or another. One could imagine that the computation that would select the right hypothesis is too long for the system to perform given available resources of memory, attention, etc.; or that the hypothesis that expresses the best hypothesis contains too many clauses (in canonical notation) for the device to parse; or that the critically relevant data base is too complex for the device to represent . . . etc. I suppose that even the most starry-eyed epistemic optimist would accept the sort of epistemic boundedness implicit in these kinds of limitations. Even if, to paraphrase Putnam (1980, p. 298), 'God chose, instead of packing our heads with a billion different mental organs, simply to make us smart', it is surely conceivable that he failed to make us *smart enough*. Perhaps solving the riddle of the universe requires one more neuron than, de facto, anyone will ever have. Sad, of course, but surely not out of the question. So I shall take it to be common ground that epistemic boundedness arising from these sorts of quantitative limitations on our cognitive capacities is compatible with the view that intelligence is general—i.e., not only with the modularity theory but with its denial.

Now let's consider some other ways in which a hypothesis-testing system could prove to be epistemically bounded; kinds of limitations that may seem to be more intimately connected with modularity per se. There are, in particular, two of these: modular systems may be supposed to be constrained in respect of the *class of hypotheses* to which they have access, and in respect of the *body of data* that can be consulted in the evaluation of any given hypothesis. The latter, according to our analysis, is a constraint that is *specific* to modular systems, since it is just a way of formulating the notion of informational encapsulation; and we have seen that it is primarily informational encapsulation that makes a system modular. Contrapositively, when we imagine a system of *general* intelligence, we are imagining a mechanism that is informationally *un*encapsulated; one in which any of the available data may be brought to bear on any of the hypotheses that it can entertain. Question: is an intelligence that is nonmodular in that sense—an informationally unencapsulated system—ipso facto epistemically unbounded?

Answer: no. The obvious reason is that epistemic unboundedness is primarily an issue about *domain specificity* and not about informational encapsulation. What epistemic unboundedness requires is that the exercise of intelligence should not be biased towards some kinds of problems to the exclusion of others; more generally, that there should be no interesting endogenous constraints on the hypotheses accessible to intelligent problem-solving. A psychology which guarantees our epistemic unboundedness would thus have to guarantee that, whatever sort of subject domain the world turns out to be, somewhere in the space of hypotheses that we are capable of entertaining there is the hypothesis that specifies its structure.

My present point is that the denial of the modularity thesis does *not* guarantee this; indeed, I don't see how any remotely plausible cognitive theory could conceivably do so. It is, in any event, patently a fallacy to suppose that since the modularity thesis implies boundedness, the way to get *un*boundedness is to deny the modularity thesis.

A good way to see what is going on here is to notice that, historically, the most nonmodular psychologies that have been proposed have nevertheless been compatible with—indeed, have entailed—very extreme versions of the boundedness thesis. Consider, e.g., the associationism of a philosopher like Hume. On Hume's view, the mind has no intrinsic architecture whatever (Hume says that the play of Ideas is like a play in a theater—except that there is no theater). There are no faculties; mental structure is reduced to parameters of association as per the discussion in Part I of this essay. And since any Idea can, in principle, become associated with any other, you have in Hume's psychology something like the ultimate in nonmodular theories of mind.

But do you have epistemic unboundedness? Not on your Nelly! In fact, the class of beliefs that can be entertained according to Hume's account is perhaps more sharply delimited than any modularity theorist has ever proposed. This is because the class of accessible *beliefs* is determined by the class of accessible *concepts*; and, for Hume, the class of accessible concepts is determined by the Empiricist principle; there are no concepts except such as can be constructed from sensations. So, in particular, if the hypotheses of the best science would be such as to make reference to God, or to electrons, or to triangles, or to mental faculties, or to any other unobservables, then the best science is humanly inaccessible on Hume's account; it is beyond the epistemic bounds that Hume posits. Moreover, and this is the consideration that cuts ice, its inaccessibility is a consequence of the (presumed) character of human psychology; if Hume is right, then it is the ontogeny of our concepts that precludes our having a science in which reference to unobservables figures ineliminably.

Of course, this isn't the way that Hume understood the epistemological consequences of his psychological views. Hume certainly does not take himself to be espousing a form of the boundedness thesis. But that is because of some *extra*psychological (roughly, semantic) theses that Hume also endorses. Hume holds more or less explicitly (and later Empiricists held absolutely explicitly) that the Empiricist principle provides a *criterion of cognitive significance*. The best science couldn't include hypotheses about God (electrons, triangles, faculties, etc.) because such hypotheses are not just psychologically *inaccessible* but also semantically *empty*. Talk about God couldn't figure in a true science because talk about God is meaningless.

The point of all this is that it's not his associationism (his nonmodularity) that buys Hume epistemic unboundedness; associationism is compatible with the most stringent constraints on the psychologically accessible beliefs. What buys Hume epistemic unboundedness is the Empiricist theory of *meaning*, a semantic thesis that has the convenient property of entailing that the psychologically inaccessible beliefs are ipso facto nontruth-valuable. If one gives up the Empiricist theory of meaning (as one must, because it is surely false), then one sees with dramatic clarity how little of epistemic unboundedness psychological nonmodularity actually guarantees.

The idea of attacking epistemic boundedness with semantic theses is, of course, still with us; for recent versions, see Davidson (1973–4) and Rorty (1979). My own view, for what it's worth, is that all such proposals are ineliminably verificationistic and hence indefensible. Very roughly, the available options seem to come in two clusters. Either one has the unintelligibility of boundedness at the price of a verificationist semantics, a coherence theory of truth and, eventually, an Idealist ontology; or one opts for Realism and correspondence at the price of making boundedness an empirical issue. I think that the second strategy is certainly the right one, but it is worth emphasizing that, in a certain sense, the modularity theory— even in a comprehensive version like Gall's—is not in jeopardy on *either* account. Suppose that some form of verificationism is true and we can make no sense of the possibility that the best science might be expressible only by hypotheses that are psychologically inaccessible to us. It could then hardly be an objection to the modularity thesis that if that possibility *were* intelligible, the modularity thesis would leave it open.

One way to get unboundedness is thus via the (slightly Pyrrhic) demonstration that its denial is unintelligible. (Slightly Pyrrhic because one is tugged by the view that if -P is unintelligible, then P must be too.) Suppose, however, that we eschew that route and assume that the issues about epistemic boundedness are empirical (though, of course, very abstractly related to data). It then seems to me hard to see how the unboundedness view can be made empirically plausible. The point is that any psychology must attribute some endogenous structure to the mind (really unstructured objects—bricks, say—don't have beliefs and desires and they don't learn things). And it's hard to see how, in the course of making such attributions of endogenous structure, the theory could fail to imply some constraints on the class of beliefs that the mind can entertain.[42] These considerations hold quite independent of issues about modularity; they suggest a sense in which *any* theory of the mind must endorse its domain specificity. The only epistemologically interesting question would thus be how likely it is that some of the inaccessible thoughts are both interesting and true.

But I don't suppose that such reflections are conclusive. Perhaps, after all, someone will some day make serious sense of an unboundedness thesis. Suffice it for present purposes to claim that nobody has been able to do so to date. All cognitive psychologies thus far proposed, modular or otherwise, imply boundedness; and some of the least modular psychologies imply some of the most drastic epistemic bounds. To repeat: when unboundedness has been defended, in the historical tradition, it has typically been on semantic rather than psychological grounds; and the semantic assumptions from which unboundedness was inferred were, in my view, uniformly not good.

If, in short, your main reason for believing in general intelligence is that you would like it to turn out that we are epistemically unbounded, then you might as well accept the modularity thesis for all the good that its denial is likely to do you. Even if cognitive processes are assumed to be uniformly Quineian and isotropic— hence utterly unencapsulated—the main argument for epistemic boundedness is still in force: so long as the class of accessible concepts is endogenously constrained, there will be thoughts that we are unequipped to think. And, so far, nobody has been able to devise an account of the ontogeny of concepts which does not imply such endogenous constraints. This conclusion may seem less unbearably depressing if one considers that it is one that we unhesitatingly accept for every *other* species. One would presumably not be impressed by a priori arguments intended to prove (e.g.) that the true science *must be* accessible to spiders.

I promised a parting word or two about what the prospects for research in cognitive science might be like assuming that the modified modularity thesis is true. My point will be this: the limits of modularity are also likely to be the limits of what we are going to be able to understand about the mind, given anything like the theoretical apparatus currently available.

Coextensions, of one sort or another, have been the burden of my plaint throughout. I have suggested that the functional distinction between input analysis and the fixation of belief divides cognitive processes at the same point as the architectural distinction between vertical and horizontal faculties; and that the distinction between vertical and horizontal faculties corresponds, in turn, to the distinction between relatively local and relatively global computations. I now add that these distinctions also demarcate the areas in which research in cognitive science has encountered some reasonable amount of success over the last twenty years or so, from those in which the failure has been pretty nearly absolute. While some interesting things have been learned about the psychology of input analysis—primarily about language and vision—the psychology of thought has proved quite intractable.

In particular, on my view, the attempt to develop general models of intelligent problem-solving—which one associates most closely with work in artificial intelligence by such figures as Schank, Minsky, Newell, Winograd, and others—has produced surprisingly little insight despite the ingenuity and seriousness with which it has often been pursued. I have the impression that it is becoming rather generally conceded that this early, as one might say Wagnerian, phase of AI research has led to a dead end, and that the direction of current interest is increasingly the simulation of relatively encapsulated processes associated with perception and language. Vision (Ullman, 1979), visual imagery (Kosslyn, 1980), and machine parsing are thus current loci of considerable activity; enthusiasm for a frontal assault on central processes—for literally building an intelligent machine—seems to have considerably abated.

What happened in much of the earlier work could be described as an (implicit) attempt to treat central processes as though they were modular. Intellectual capacities were divided into what seem, in retrospect, to be quite arbitrary subdepartments (proving theorems of elementary logic; pushing blocks around; ordering hamburgers), and the attempted simulations proceeded by supplying machines with very large amounts of more or less disorganized, highly topic-specific facts and heuristics. The result was an account of central processes which failed to capture precisely what is most interesting about them: their wholism, what we have been calling their Quineianism and isotropy. What emerged was a picture of the mind that looked rather embarrassingly like a Sears catalogue.[43]

Precisely analogous remarks hold for cognitive science outside AI. What has been reasonably successfully developed is a sort of extended psychophysics. A lot is known about the transformations of representations which serve to get information into a form appropriate for central processing; practically nothing is known about what happens after the information gets there. The ghost has been chased further back into the machine, but it has not been exorcised.

I won't argue for this evaluation of the present state of the art; I am fully aware that it's tendentious. What I do want to argue for is this: if the modified modularity theory is true, it is not unintelligible that our successes and failures should have been distributed in the way I've just described. Specifically, if central processes have the sorts of properties that I have ascribed to them, then they are bad candidates for scientific study.

One relatively minor reason is this. We have seen that isotropic systems are unlikely to exhibit articulated neuroarchitecture. If, as seems plausible, neuroarchitecture is often a concomitant of constraints on information flow, then neural equipontentiality is what you would expect in systems in which every process has more or less uninhibited access to all the available data. The moral is that, to the extent that the existence of form/function correspondence is a precondition for successful neuropsychological research, there is not much to be expected in the way of a neuropsychology of thought. The analogy to computers looks to be revealing here: The more specialized the machine, the more its physical architecture is likely to mirror the structure of its computations; whereas, in the general purpose machine, form/function correspondence tends to be less striking, and instantaneous computational structure is determined by the details of the program being run. At the extreme of this continuum are fully general systems like Turing machines, where fixed architecture is, to all intents and purposes, nonexistent. If, as philosophers speculated for a while, the optimal model of the brain were as a realized Turing machine, one would, of course, expect there to be no serious science of neuropsychology. The present point is that any account of central processes as Quineian and isotropic also tends in that direction.

There are, however, much deeper grounds for gloom. The fact is that—considerations of their neural realization to one side—global systems are per se bad domains for computational models, at least of the sorts that cognitive scientists are accustomed to employ. The condition for successful science (in physics, by the way, as well as psychology) is that nature should have joints to carve it at: relatively simple subsystems which can be artificially isolated and which behave, in isolation, in something like the way that they behave *in situ*. Modules satisfy this condition; Quineian/isotropic-wholistic-systems by definition do not. If, as I have supposed, the central cognitive processes are nonmodular, that is very bad news for cognitive science.

Localness, to put it the other way around, is a leading characteristic of the sorts of computations that we know how to think about. Consider, once again, the situation in the philosophy of science, where we can see the issues about fixation of belief writ large. Here an interesting contrast is between deductive logic—the history of which is, surely, one of the great success stories of human inquiry—and confirmation theory which, by fairly general consensus, is a field that mostly does not exist. My point is that this asymmetry, too, is likely no accident. Deductive logic is the theory of validity, and validity is a *local* property of sentences. Roughly, the idea is that the validity of a sentence is determined given a specification of its logical form, and the logical form of a sentence is determined given a specification of its vocabulary and syntax. In this respect, the validity of a sentence contrasts starkly with its level of confirmation, since the latter, as we have seen, is highly sensitive to global properties of belief systems.[44] It is not surprising that philosophers discussing confirmation often resort to metaphors of interacting fields of forces; just as Gestalt psychologists did when they worried about wholistic effects in cognition. The problem in both cases is to get the structure of an entire belief system to bear on individual occasions of belief fixation. We have, to put it bluntly, no computational formalisms that show us how to do this, and we have no idea how such formalisms might be developed.

I am suggesting that the reason why there is no serious psychology of central cognitive processes is the same as the reason why there is no serious philosophy of scientific confirmation. Both exemplify the significance of global factors in the fixation of belief, and nobody begins to understand how such factors have their effects. In this respect, cognitive science hasn't even *started*; we are literally no farther advanced than we were in the darkest days of behaviorism (though we are, no doubt, in some beneficent respects more disillusioned). If someone—a Dreyfus, for example—were to ask us why we should even suppose that the digital computer is a plausible mechanism for the simulation of global cognitive processes, the answering silence would be deafening.

The moral, I suppose, is that it would be rational to pray that Gall was at least a little right; that there are at least some cognitive systems that are sufficiently modular—hence sufficiently local in their computational character—that they can be studied prior to the development of theories of the effects of global determinants in belief fixation. That our cognitive science has got anywhere at all suggests that this prayer may have been answered. Modified rapture!

Notes

1. It may be worth while, before we leave this topic, to point out that Chomsky's talk of mental organs somewhat unilluminates the history of doctrinal relations between orthodox Cartesianism and faculty psychologists. Real (as opposed to *Neo-*) Cartesians were quite often *opponents* of faculty theorizing, which they held (perhaps correctly) to be incompatible with a due acknowledgment of the metaphysical unity of the soul. One might, therefore, be surprised to find faculty psychology endorsed by avowed followers in the Cartesian footsteps. However, as we have seen, what the Neocartesians mean by a mental organ—viz., a body of innate *propositional attitudes*—is not what real Cartesians meant by (and denounced as) mental faculties—viz., functionally individuated psychological *mechanisms*. You need to bear this distinction in mind if you want a clear view of how current drifts of theory relate to their traditional sources. Can't see the game without a program.

2. I'm not at all sure, by the way, that Harris' reading of Locke is right in this respect. The direction of Locke's thought on these matters seems to have been away from faculty psychology and toward a doctrine of intrinsic mental *capacities* or dispositions. The postulation of these latter he appears to have viewed as, as it were, explanatory bedrock; specifically, the exercise of such mental "powers" is *not* viewed—even implicitly—as mediated by a corresponding apparatus of psychological mechanisms. (Shades of Gilbert Ryle.) Thus Locke says about memory that "this laying up of our ideas in the repository of memory signifies no more but this—that the mind has a power, in many cases, to revive perceptions which it once had . . ." (Locke, *Essay*, Book 2, chapter 10, par. 2). It is of interest that this positivistic disclaimer was new in the second edition of the *Essay*, talk of a "repository to lay up . . . Ideas" having been unabashed in the earlier version of the text. This rather suggests (contrary to Harris) that the incompatibility, at least in spirit, between a thoroughgoing Empiricism and any acknowledgment of endogenous psychological mechanisms was becoming clear to Locke. On this reading, Locke was far from viewing the existence of "natural faculties" as "too obvious to mention," anathema having been, at least by the second edition of the *Essay*, fairly explicitly pronounced.

3. It may be worth reemphasizing that the *non*cartesian faculty psychologist need not be an *anti*cartesian faculty psychologist. On the contrary, it is perfectly possible to take the view that the typical cognitive faculty is a mechanism for the manipulation of mental representations. These latter may in turn be viewed as endowed with propositional contents, hence as vehicles for encoding the informational structures with which Neocartesian theories are primarily concerned. Most serious contemporary cognitive science is, I think, committed to some such account. More of this later.

4. Spearman (1927, p. 29) lists seven mental faculties which he claims were traditionally acknowledged: sense, intellect, memory, imagination, attention, speech, and movement. "Any further increase in the number of faculties beyond these seven has, in general, only been attained by subdividing some or other of these." Of the faculties enumerated in Spearman's census, only the first five are clearly 'horizontal' in the sense of the present discussion, and 'speech' is a vertical faculty par excellence. This sort of indifference to the horizontal/vertical distinction is, by the way, practically universal in the faculty psychology literature, Franz Joseph Gall being, as we shall see, perhaps the only major figure to insist upon it.

    Spearman's views on the history of psychology will, by the way, be frequently referred to in what follows; he is the one major experimental psychologist in this century to take the faculty tradition seriously.

5. Plato also has a quite different story (an epistemological one, elaborately set forth in The *Republic*) according to which faculties are to be distinguished by reference to the ontological status of their objects: belief is directed toward Appearance, knowledge toward Reality, and so forth. I'm not sure how these two accounts of the faculties are supposed to fit together, but if Plato was the first philosopher to have trouble squaring his psychology with his epistemology, he was by no means the last. John Marshall (personal communication) reminds me that Aquinas required faculties to be individuated *both* with respect to their

objects *and* with respect to their mode of functioning ("per actus et objecta"), but with the functional criteria having precedence; this last indicative, presumably, of Aristotelian (as opposed to Platonic) allegiances.

6. See Marshall (1980). It was Marshall's article that first put me on to Gall, and I have used the same sources for Gall's material that Marshall quotes. As must by now be apparent, however, I'm impressed by some of the differences between Gall's theory and that of latter-day organologists like Chomsky; to this extent my reading of the texts differs from Marshall's. Marshall is, however, certainly right in seeing in Gall's view that the brain is a *collection* of organs a clear foreshadowing of some of Chomsky's favorite claims. Chomsky and Gall mean rather different things by "faculty"; but that faculties are typically endogenously specified and domain specific are points on which they agree.

7. There are other unsatisfactory aspects of (what I take to be) Gall's implicit analogy between inherited parameters of individual difference on the one hand and instincts on an other. So, to stick with the example in the text, even if an aptitude for playing good baseball is inherited, it isn't an *isolated* aptitude in the way that bird song is. Whereas really fine baseball players are likely to be pretty good at golf and lacrosse, birds are idiot savants in respect of their ability to sing their species song; no lark has even an amateur talent for madrigals.

Gall himself tacitly acknowledges that some of his vertical faculties aren't, in this sense, 'isolated', but rather fall into families of related capacities—e.g., that mathematical and musical aptitude may have something interesting in common. In such cases, Gall often postulates adjacent centers in the brain. However, since neural propinquity doesn't have any very natural psychological interpretation in Gall's theory, this would seem to be little more than a cop-out; an occasional attempt to get the force of a horizontal taxonomy in the context of what is vehemently asserted to be a strictly vertical functional architecture.

8. This puts the case a little too strongly. Gall does, of course, think there are functional homologies between, say, mathematical memory and musical memory; both mediate the recall of things. The two memory systems are, however, supposed to be distinct by neurological criteria and by the criterion of autonomy of operation.

9. Even this may overestimate the similarity between Gall's views and Chomsky's. Gall doesn't actually seem to be very interested in innate *information*, the major burden of his plaint being the existence of innate *mental capacities*. As we've seen, it takes a special—Cartesian—view of how mental capacities are to be explained to see the second of these issues as crucially involving the first.

10. "Phrenology's fundamental assumptions remained constant throughout the history of the movement. They were succinctly stated by George Combe as consisting of the folowing three 'fundamental principles': (1) That the brain is the organ of the mind; (2) That the brain is the aggregate of several parts, each subserving a distinct mental faculty; (3) That the size of the cerebral organ is, ceteris paribus, an index of power or energy of function" (Bynum, 1976). See also Critchley (1979): "As originally put forward, there were four cardinal premises (of phrenology), namely that: (1) the brain is the material instrument through which the mind holds intercourse with the outer world; (2) the mind entails a congeries of discrete mental faculties each with its own specific center or organ; (3) the

size of each organ corresponds with the functional efficiency of each faculty; and (4) the development of the organ is reflected in the shape, size and irregularities of the encompassing cranium."

11. Among classical associationists, the German philosopher/psychologist Herbart seems to have been unusually explicit in viewing a dynamics of mental contents as an alternative to the traditional apparatus of faculties *cum* mechanisms: "psychological phenomena are to be explained as due to the combination and interactions of certain ultimate mental states (presentations: *vorstellungen*) to the exclusion of everything of the nature of innate ideas, faculties, or activities" (Stout, 1930, p. 5). What primarily distinguishes Herbart from the British associationists is that, while both held a psychology based upon the quasimechanical attraction, exclusion, and assimilation of mental representations, he also held a metaphysical view of the soul as simple and unchanging. Herbart can thus be seen as simultaneously endorsing the Empiricist *and* Cartesian objections to faculty psychology. His was not, perhaps, the most stable of polemical positions.

12. Strictly speaking, I suppose, a convention must be something one can adhere to if one chooses; so perhaps the principle at issue is not "Say only what is true" but rather "Say only what you believe." General adherence to the latter injunction will license inferences from utterances to how the world is, given the assumption (which is, anyhow, in all sorts of ways epistemologically indispensable) that much of what people believe is true.

13. The "McGurk effect" provides fairly clear evidence for cross-modal linkages in at least one input system for the modularity of which there is independent evidence. McGurk has demonstrated that what are, to all intents and purposes, hallucinatory speech sounds can be induced when the subject is presented with a visual display of a speaker making vocal gestures appropriate to the production of those sounds. The suggestion is that (within, presumably, narrowly defined limits) mechanisms of phonetic analysis can be activated by—and can apply to—*either* accoustic *or* visual stimuli. (See McGurk and MacDonald, 1976). It is of central importance to realize that the McGurk effect—though cross-modal—is itself domain specific—viz., specific to language. A motion picture of a bouncing ball does not induce bump, bump, bump hallucinations. (I am indebted to Professor Alvin Liberman both for bringing McGurk's results to my attention and for his illuminating comments on their implications.)

14. Generally speaking, the more peripheral a mechanism is in the process of perceptual analysis—the earlier it operates, for example—the better candidate for modularity it is likely to be. In the limit, it is untendentious—even traditional—to view the functioning of psychophysical (/sensory) mechanisms as largely autonomous with respect to central processes and largely parallel with respect to one another.

There is recent, striking evidence owing to Treisman and her colleagues that the detection of such stimulus "features" as shape and color is typically parallel, preattentive, and *prior* to the identification of the object in which the features, as it were, inhere: ". . . features are registered early, automatically, and in parallel across the visual field, while objects are identified separately only at a later stage, which requires focused attention" (Treisman and Gelade, 1980, p. 98). There is analogous evidence for the modularity of phonetic feature detectors that operate in speech perception (see Eimas and Corbet, 1973), though its interpretation is less than univocal (see Ganong, 1977).

15. I won't, in general, have much to say about input processes other than those involved in vision and language, since these are by far the areas in which the available psychology is most developed. But I hope, and believe, that the points I'll be making apply pretty well to all of the perceptual mechanisms.

16. Strictly speaking, I suppose I should say that this is true according to all current non-Gibsonian accounts. For reasons given elsewhere, however (see Fodor and Pylyshyn, 1981), I am deeply unmoved by the Gibsonian claim to have devised a noncomputational theory of perception. I propose simply to ignore it in this discussion.

17. Also, given that you hear it as speech, you may have some (surely very limited) options as to which speech you hear it as. For a demonstration of instructional effects in phone recognition, see Carden, Levitt, Jusczyk, and Walley (1981). In somewhat similar fashion: it's hard to see the Necker cube in anything but three-dimensional projection; but you do have some control over which three-dimensional projection you see.

18. Pedantic footnote: To the best of my knowlege, the suggestion that what seems to be the inaccessibility of information to *consciousness* is in fact just its inaccessibility to *recall* was first made by William James in the *Principles of Psychology*. James, in his enthusiasm, takes this claim to be quite general. If he'd been right, then the specific inaccessibility of intermediate input representations to report would be a relatively uninteresting epiphenomenon of the subject's allocation of memory resources. However, as we shall see, James's story won't wash; there is clearly more to unconsciousness than he supposed.

19. A similar moral is suggested by studies of 'compressed' speech, in which signals presented at input rates much in excess of normal are apparently quite intelligible so long as the increased speed is not achieved at the price of acoustic degradation of the signal. (See Foulke, 1971.)

20. A sufficient, but not a necessary, condition for the level of representation n being 'higher' than the level of representation m is that the entities specified at n contain the entities specified at m as constituents (in the way that words have syllables as constituents, for example). It would be nice if there proved to be a well-ordering of the interlevels of representation computed by each input system, but nothing in the present discussion depends on assuming that this is so. Still less is there reason to assume, in cases where the computations that a system performs are affected by data fed into it from outside, that the exogenous information can always be ordered, with respect to abstractness, relative to the levels of representation that the system computes. I shall conform to the prevalent usage in which *all* effects of background beliefs and expectations in perceptual processing are described as the feedback of information from 'higher levels'. But it is far from clear that either 'higher' or 'level' should be taken very seriously when so employed.

21. A corollary consideration is that, if the argument for expectation-driven processes

in perception is to be made on teleological grounds, their putative advantages must be carefully weighed against their likely costs. In cases where the environment does *not* exhibit the expected redundancy, the typical effect of predictive error will be to *interfere with* the correct analysis (see Posner, 1978). It is thus by no means a trivial matter to show—even in cases like language processing where quantitative estimates of redundancy can, in some respects, be achieved— that the balance of payoffs favors predictive mechanisms over ones that are data driven. (See Gough, Alford, and Haley-Wilcox, 1978.)

22. That is, perceptual categories are not, in general, *definable* in terms of transducer outputs; phenomenalists, operationalists, Gibsonians, and procedural semanticists to the contrary notwithstanding. (See Fodor, 1981, chap. 7; Fodor and Pylyshyn, 1981.)

23. A plausible inference from this discussion is that lots of information to which input analyzers do have access must be stored twice; once internal to the input analyzers and once in the (putative) central memory where it is accessible to nonmodular cognitive processes. This seems natural enough: when you learn about English syntax (e.g., in a linguistics course), what you are learning is something that, in some sense, you already knew. See the discussion of 'sub-doxastic' belief at the end of this section.

24. It might be suggested that the impressive consideration is not that there is sometimes measurable competition between input systems, but that the decrements in performance that such competition produces are so small. Given the amount of processing that each must involve, the very fact that we can speak and see at the same time is, arguably, enough to vindicate Gall. But nobody knows what the null hypothesis would look like here, and given the impossibility of serious quantitative estimates, I don't propose to press the point.

25. Recent experiments increasingly suggest that the effects of contextual variables upon the identification of words in sentences are far more fragile than psychologists of the top-down persuasion used to suppose. For example, if you ask a subject to decide, at his best speed, whether a stimulus item is a word (i.e., as opposed to a phonologically licit nonsense syllable), then he will be faster for a word that is highly predictable in context than for that same word in a neutral context. In effect, 'salt' is faster in 'pepper and ——' than in 'cheese and ——'. This makes it look as though contextual predictability is facilitating 'lexical decision' and is just the sort of result that is grist for the New Look psychologist's mill. It turns out, however, that if you compare reaction times for a highly-predictable-in-context word with reaction times for that same word *in isolation*, you find no facilitation at all when the Cloze probability of the former stimulus is less than 90 percent (Fishler and Bloom, 1979). It appears, in light of such findings, that previous claims for the cognitive penetration of lexical access by contextual information may have been considerably exaggerated. At best, the phenomenon seems to be sensitive to the choice of experimental paradigm and of baseline.

26. A proposal currently in the air is to split the difference between strictly encapsulated parsers and contextually driven ones, as follows: semantic information is never used to predict syntactic structure, but a line of analysis on which the

parser is engaged can be aborted whenever it produces structures that resist contextual integration. Boxologically, this means that the parser feeds information freely to the context analyzer, but all that the context analyzer is allowed to say to the parser is either 'yes' (continue with the present line of analysis) or 'no' (try something else, I can't fit what you're giving me to the context). What the context analyzer is *prohibited* from doing is telling the parser *which* line of analysis it ought to try next—i.e., semantic information can't be used predictively to guide the parse. (For a discussion of this model, see Crain and Steedman, 1981.) All the results I know on context effects in parsing are compatible with this account; I'm inclined to bet (small denominations) that something of the sort will prove to be true.

27. Stich himself speaks not of subdoxastic beliefs but of subdoxastic *states*, not only to avoid etymological solecism, but also to emphasize that the subdoxastic lacks some of belief's paradigm properties. Granting Stich's point, the present terminology is nonetheless convenient and I shall adhere to it.

28. Perhaps it goes without saying that any mechanism which assigns linguistic tokens to linguistic types will have to know not just a lot about the tokens but also a lot about the types. I assume that something like a representation of a grammar for L must be contained in any system that is able to compute the token-to-type relation for L. Since the grammar is presumed to be represented *internal* to the sentence analyzer, the accessibility of grammatical information to that system does *not* constitute a violation of its informational encapsulation.

29. It may, indeed, do less. Hilary Putnam has the following poser. Lincoln said, "You can fool all of the people some of the time." Did he mean *there is a time at which you can fool all of the people* or did he mean *for each person there is a time at which you can fool him*? Putnam thinks that Lincoln's intentions may have been *indeterminate* as between these readings. This could, of course, be true only if the specification of quantifier scope is not mandatory in the internal representation of one's intended utterances. And *that* could be true only if such representations *do not* specify the logical form of the intended utterance. To put it another way, on Putnam's view, the internal representation of "You can fool all of the people some of the time" would be something like "You can fool all of the people some of the time," this latter being a *univocal* formula which happens to have disjoint truth conditions. Whether Putnam is right about all this remains to be seen; but if he is, then perhaps the specifically *linguistic* processes in the production/perception of speech deploy representations that are *shallower* than logical forms.

30. There has been a good deal of confusion on this point in the psychological literature. For example, some arguments of Marslen-Wilson and Tyler's (1982) seem to presuppose that it is a condition on the psychological reality of a linguistic level (hence on the truth of a grammar which postulates the level) that all items at that level should all be recognized by one and the same perceptual processor. But this is surely not required. For example, it would not prejudice the claim that English sentences decompose into words if it turned out that there were several different word recognizers—e.g., one for long words and one for short ones; or, less fancifully, one for closed-class words and one for

open-class ones (see Garrett, 1982). It's nice when the levels that your grammar requires in order to say what linguistic types the language contains turn out to correspond to the outputs that some single processor computes. But neither the theory of grammar nor the theory of processing requires that this be so.

31. It may be thought Pickwickian, after all that we've been through together, for me to cleave to phenomenological accessibility as a criterion of the output of the visual processor. I must confess to being influenced, in part, by ulterior— specifically, epistemological—motives. It seems to me that we want a notion of perceptual process that makes the deliverances of perception available as the premises of *conscious* decisions and inferences; for it seems to me indubitable that, e.g., it sometimes happens that I look out the window, see that it is raining, and decide, in light of what I see, to carry my umbrella. If we allow that the deliverances of the visual input system are *very* shallow representations (edges and colors, say), then we shall have to hold either that input analysis is a very much less rich process than perceiving—mere psychophysics, in effect—or that the intuition that one *sees* such things as that it's raining—and the rain—is misled. Since I feel no inclination towards either of these alternatives, I want a vocabulary for the output of the visual processor which specifies stimulus properties that are phenomenologically accessible and that are, by preference, reasonably close to those stimulus properties that we pretheoretically suppose to be visible.

"Ah, ha," you reply, "but haven't you cautioned us, repeatedly, *not* to confuse input-processing with the fixation of perceptual belief? And isn't that confusion implicit in the preceding?" Well, it's true that the fixation of belief, perceptual or otherwise, is a central process (since what one believes is sensitive to what one takes to be the state of the evidence *überhaupt*, including the beliefs previously arrived at). I am supposing that input systems offer central processes hypotheses about the world, such hypotheses being responsive to the current, local distribution of proximal stimulations. The evaluation of these hypotheses in light of the rest of what one knows is one of the things that central processes are for; indeed, it *is* the fixation of perceptual belief. However, this picture does not constrain the, as it were, vocabulary in which such hypotheses are couched. It leaves open the issue—essential to the modularity thesis—of the level of abstraction at which the interface between input analyzers and central systems occurs. I am now suggesting that, barring evidence to the contrary, it would be convenient if the output vocabulary of the perceptual analyzers overlapped the vocabulary of such (prima facie) perceptual premises as figure in conscious inference and decision-making (so that such remarks as 'I see that it's raining" could be taken as literally true and not just enthymemic). Why shouldn't one assume what it is convenient to assume?

32. Since dogs are prototypical animals, most of the properties that *animal* elicits will also be assigned to *dog*. The fact cited in the text is, however, independent of this consideration; it is a function of the basicness of the category, not of its prototypicality.

33. I'm making it easy for myself by assuming that visual transducers detect shape, color, local motion, etc. "directly"; which, of course, they do not. Presumably,

the real psychophysical parameters are very low-level indeed (reflectances and visual frequencies, e.g.), shape, color . . . etc. being inferred from these psychophysical parameters and represented at interlevels of input analysis. Basic categorizations are, in turn, inferred from the interlevel representations. Need one add that it is very important to the whole shape of one's theory of perception what one takes the true psychophysical parameters to be? Or that that determination must be made on the basis of empirical considerations and not at the convenience of a foundationalist epistemology? (For discussion, see Fodor and Pylyshyn, op. cit.)

34. Marr and Nishihara (1978) suggest that the interface between "geometric" and "conceptual" representations of the visual stimulus (the process that psychologists call "object identification") takes place at the level of the "3 D sketch." This representation specifies the distal object as an organization, in three dimensions, of components each of which is in turn characterized by "1) its average location (or center of mass); 2) its overall size, as exemplified by its mean diameter or volume; and 3) its principal axis of elongation or symmetry, if one exists" (p. 37). The spatial arrangement of these components is specified by reference to object-centered (as opposed to observer-centered) coordinates.

From our point of view, the main interest of 3 D sketch representations lies in the conjecture that they can be computed, more or less algorithmically, from a specification of such primitive information as sequences of retinal mosaics. The work of Marr and his colleagues has been sufficiently successful that it is possible to take that conjecture as more than just wishful thinking. If it is, in fact, true, then we can imagine that the final stage of visual input analysis involves accessing a 'form-concept' dictionary which, in effect, pairs 3 D sketches with basic categories. To develop such a model would be to show, in detail, how an informationally encapsulated visual processor could perform object identification at the basic category level. That would make modularity theorists *very* happy.

35. I want to be quite clear what is—and what is not—implied by talk of modular systems "sharing a cluster of properties." One interpretation might be this: Given that a system has any of the properties in question, then the likelihood is considerable that it has all of the rest. However, I doubt that a claim that strong could be empirically sustained, since it is reasonably easy to think of psychological processes that are fast but not encapsulated, or involuntary but not innate, and so forth. The present contention, in any event, is relatively modest; it's that if a psychological system has *most* of the modularity properties, then it is very likely to have *all* of them. This claim does not imply that only modular systems are fast, or involuntary, or encapsulated . . . etc. But it *is* alleged to be characteristic of modular systems to have all of these traits at once.

36. This is, of course, an idealization; decisions about what to believe (subdoxastically or otherwise) do not, in general, succeed in making the optimal use of the available data. This consideration does not, however, affect the present point, which is just that such decisions must, of necessity, be sensitive to information from many different sources.

37. There is an assumption underlying this line of argument which the reader may

not wish to grant: that the mechanisms that interface between vertical faculties have to be *computational* rather than, as one might say, merely mechanical. Old views of how language connects with perception (e.g., percepts are pictures and words are their associates) implicitly deny this assumption. It seems to me, however, that anyone who thinks seriously about what must be involved in deciding (e.g.) how to say what we see will accept the plausibility of the view that the mental processes that are implicated must be both computational and of formidable complexity.

38. Stronger versions had it that each theory statement must be logically equivalent to some (finite?) conjunction of observation statements. For a sophisticated review of this literature, see Glymour, 1980. Glymour takes exception to some aspects of the Quineian account of confirmation, but not for reasons that need concern us here.

39. It is often proposed (see, e.g., McCarthy, 1980) that a logic capable of coping with the frame problem will have to be 'nonmonotonic'. (Roughly, a logic is monotonic when the addition of new postulates does *not* reduce the set of previously derivable theorems; nonmonotonic otherwise.) The point is that new beliefs don't just get *added on* to the old set; rather, old beliefs are variously altered to accommodate the new ones. This is, however, hardly surprising on the analysis of the frame problem proposed in the text. For, on that account, the frame problem is not distinguishable from the problem of nondemonstrative confirmation, and confirmation relations are themselves typically nonmonotonic. For example, the availability of a new datum may necessitate the assignment of new confirmation levels to indefinitely many previously accepted hypotheses. Hence, if we think of the confirmation system as formalized, indefinitely many previously derivable formulas of the form 'the level of H is L' may become nontheorems whenever new data become available.

40. Since there is no particular relation between *the frame problem* and *frames*-cum-data structures, the nomenclature in this area could hardly be more confusing.

41. The localization dispute didn't, of course, end with Gall and Flourens. For a useful, brief survey of its relatively modern history (since Wernicke), see Eggert (1977). It is of some interest—in passing—that Wernicke, committed localizationalist though he was in respect of the language mechanisms, held that only "primary functions . . . can be referred to specific areas. . . . All processes which exceed these primary functions (such as the synthesis of various perceptions into concepts and the complex functions such as thought and consciousness) are dependent upon the fiber bundles connecting different areas of the cortex" (p. 92). Barring the associationism, Wernicke's picture is not very different from the one that we've been developing here.

42. The traditional way of resolving this difficulty is to infer the *universality* of thought from its *immateriality*—on the principle, apparently, that ectoplasm can do anything. Here is Geach's exposition of Aquinas' treatment: "Aquinas . . . holds that a thought consists in the *nonmaterial* occurrence of a form of nature. . . . There can on this view be no special nature of the thought process to be discovered empirically; such a special nature might be expected to impose restrictions on what can be thought of, as a colored glass does on what can be

seen through it—and Aquinas regards this sort of restriction as evidently impossible. Whatever nature of thing an A may be, if there can be an A there can be a thought of an A. . . . For if it is not impossible for there to be something of the nature A, then there can be something of that nature existing with *esse naturale* (viz., 'in the world'), and, equally, there can be something of the nature existing with *esse intentionale* (viz., as an 'object of thought'). . . . It is only when the *esse* is not merely intentional, but also freed from the limitation of matter, that we have an unrestricted possibility of the occurrence, by that kind of *esse*, of whatever natures can occur in reality at all" (1961, pp. 96–97). The point here is not, of course, just that if A makes sense, so too does *the thought of A*. It's rather that, on the assumption that thought is immaterial, there are no empirical (no nonlogical) constraints on what we can think about. The question raised in the text is whether the universality of thought is plausible on any *other* ontological assumption.

43. That this account of the recent history of AI is not entirely eccentric can be seen by comparing Allport (1980), who, however, draws a quite different moral from the one I have endorsed. Allport is explicit in viewing much of AI as the attempt to treat what I've been calling central processes on the model of modularized systems of production rules. Allport cites (inter alia) the research of Anderson, Schank, Newell, and Winograd as indicating the promise of this approach. I am in agreement with Allport's description of the research but not with his evaluation of it. On the contrary, I take it that the bankruptcy of this sort of AI is self-evident and constitutes a strong prima facie argument that the organization of central processes is, in fact, not modular.

44. I am, of course, distinguishing between the theory of confirmation, which doesn't exist, and the theory of statistical probability, which certainly does. Like deductive logic, probability theory is about a *local* relation—one which holds between a hypothesis and an *antecedently delimited* body of data. Since the theory gives no general account of what it is for data to be relevant to the assessment of a hypothesis, or of how the acceptability of a hypothesis varies as a function of the simplicity, plausibility, conservatism . . . etc. of competing hypotheses, there can be no demonstrative inference from statistical significance to level of confirmation. Notice that this is *not* just because significantly skewed distributions of data sometimes occur by chance. It is for the much deeper reason that the confirmation of a hypothesis is sensitive to considerations for which probability theory provides no metric.

REFERENCES

Allport, D. (1980), "Patterns And Actions, Cognitive Mechanisms Are Content Specific," in G. Claxton (ed.), *Cognitive Psychology: New Directions*. London, Routledge & Kegan Paul.

Anglin, J. (1979), *The Growth of Word Meaning*, Cambridge, Mass., MIT Press.

Anscombe, G., and Geach, P. (1967), *Three Philosophers*, Oxford, Blackwell.

Bartlett, F. (1932), *Remembering: A Study in Experimental and Social Psychology*, Cambridge, England, Cambridge University Press.

Berlin, B., and Kay, P. (1969), *Basic Color Terms: Their Universality and Evolution*, Berkeley, University of California Press.

Bizzi, E. (1968), "Discharge of Frontal Eye Field Neurons during Saccadic and Following Eye Movements in Unanesthetized Monkeys," *Experimental Brain Research*, 6:69–80.

Block, N. (1980), "What Is Functionalism?" in N. Block (ed.), *Readings in Philosophy of Psychology*, Cambridge, Mass., Harvard University Press.

Bower, T. (1974) *Development in Infancy*, San Francisco, W. H. Freeman.

Bransford, J., Barclay, J., and Franks, J. (1972), "Sentence Memory: A Constructive versus Interpretive Approach," *Cognitive Psychology*, 3:193–209.

Brooks, L. (1968), "Spatial And Verbal Components of the Act of Recall," *Canadian Journal of Psychology*, 22:349–368.

Brown, R. (1958), "How Shall a Thing Be Called?" *Psychological Review*, 65:14–21.

Brown, R. (1973) *A First Language: The Early Stages*, Cambridge, Mass., Harvard University Press.

Bruner, J. (1957), "On Perceptual Readiness," *Psychological Review*, 64:123–152.

Bynum, W. (1976), "Varieties of Cartesian Experience in Early Nineteenth Century Neurophysiology," in S. Spicker and H. Engelhardt, *Philosophical Dimensions of the Neuro-Medical Sciences*, Dodrecht, Reidel.

Caplan, D. (1981), "Comments on J. A. Fodor, "The Modularity of Mind," unpublished paper presented at the Conference on Foundations of Cognitive Science, University of Western Ontario.

Carden, G., Levitt, A., Jusczyk, P., and Walley, A. (1981), "Evidence for Phonetic Processing of Cues to Place of Articulation: Perceived Manner Affects Perceived Place," *Perception and Psychophysics*, 29,1:26–36.

Carey, S. (1978), "A Case Study: Face Recognition," in E. Walker (ed.), *Explorations in the Biology of Language*, Cambridge, Mass., MIT Press.

Carey, S., and Diamond, R. (1980), "Maturational Determination of the Developmental Course of Face Encoding," in D. Caplan (ed.), *Biological Studies of Mental Processes*, Cambridge, Mass., MIT Press.

Carnap, R. (1960), *Meaning and Necessity*, Chicago, University of Chicago Press.

Chomsky, N. (1965), *Aspects of the Theory of Syntax*, Cambridge, Mass., MIT Press.

Chomsky, N. (1980), "Rules And Representations," *The Behavorial and Brain Sciences*, 3:1–15.

Chomsky, N. (1982), *Lectures on Government and Binding*, Foris Publications, Dodrecht.

Collins, A., and Loftus, E. (1975), "A Spreading-Activation Theory of Semantic Processing," *Psychological Review*, 82:407–428.

Corteen, R., and Wood, B. (1972), "Autonomic Responses to Shock-Associated Words in an Unattended Channel," *Journal of Experimental Psychology*, 94.308–313.

Crain, S., and Steedman, M. (1981), "On Not Being Led Up the Garden Path: The Use of Context by the Psychological Parser," Paper presented at the Sloan Conference on Human Parsing, University of Texas, Austin.

Critchley, M. (1979), *The Divine Banquet of the Brain*, New York, Raven Press.

Crowder, R., and Morton, J. (1969), "Precategorical Acoustic Storage (PAS)," *Perception and Psychophysics*, 5.365–373.

Davidson, D. (1973-4), "On the Very Idea of a Conceptual Scheme," *Proceedings and Addresses of the American Philosophical Association*, 67:5–20.

De Groot, A. (1965), *Thought and Choice in Chess*, The Hague, Mouton.

Dretske, F. (1981), *Knowledge and the Flow of Information*, Cambridge, Mass., MIT Press.

Eggert, G. (1977), *Wernicke's Works on Aphasia: A Sourcebook and Review*, The Hague, Mouton.

Eimas, P., and Corbit, J. (1973), "Selective Adaptation of Linguistic Feature Detectors," *Cognitive Psychology*, 4:99–109.

Fishler, I., and Bloom, P. (1980), "Rapid Processing of the Meaning of Sentences," *Memory and Cognition*, 8,3:216–225.

Fodor, J. (1965), *Psychological Explanation*, New York, Random House.

Fodor, J. (1975), *The Language of Thought*, New York, Thomas Y. Crowell.

Fodor, J. (1981), *Representations*, Cambridge, Mass., MIT Press.

Fodor, J. (1981), "The Mind-Body Problem," *Scientific American*, 244,1:124–133.

Fodor, J. (forthcoming) "Psychosemantics, or: Where Do Truth Conditions Come From?"

Fodor, J., Bever, T., and Garrett, M. (1974), *The Psychology of Language*, New York, McGraw-Hill.

Fodor, J., Fodor, J., and Garrett, M. (1975), "The Psychological Unreality of Semantic Representations," *Linguistic Inquiry*, 6,4:515–531.

Fodor, J., Garrett, M., Walker, E., and Parkes, C. (1980), "Against Definitions," *Cognition*, 8:263–367.

Fodor, J., and Pylyshyn, Z. (1981), "How Direct Is Visual Perception?" *Cognition*, 9:139–196.

Forster, K., and Olbrei, I. (1973), "Semantic Heuristics and Syntactic Analysis," *Cognition*, 2:319–347.

Foss, D. (1969), "Decision Processes during Sentence Comprehension: Effects of Lexical Item Difficulty and Position upon Decision Times," *Journal of Verbal Learning and Verbal Behavior*, 8:457–462.

Foulke, E. (1971), "The Perception of Time Compressed Speech," in D. Horton and J. Jenkins (eds.), *The Perception of Language*, Ohio, Charles E. Merrill.

Frazier, L., and Fodor, J. D. (1978), "The Sausage Machine: A New Two-Stage Parsing Model," *Cognition*, 6,4:291–325.

Gall, F. (See Hollander, B.)

Gardner, M. (1952), *In the Name of Science*, New York, Putnam.

Ganong, W. (1977), "Selective Adaptation and Speech Perception," Ph.D. thesis, M.I.T.

Garrett, M. (1982), "A Perspective on Research in Language Production," in G. Mehler, E. Walker, and M. Garrett (eds.), *Perspectives on Mental Representation*, Hillsdale, N.J., Lawrence Erlbaum Associates.

Geach, P. (1967), "Aquinas," in G. Anscombe and P. Geach, *Three Philosophers*, q.v.

Gleitman, L. (1981), "Maturational Determinants of Language Growth," *Cognition*, 10:103–114.

Glymour, C. (1980), *Theory and Evidence*, Princeton, Princeton University Press.

Goldin-Meadow, S., and Feldman, H. (1977), "The Development of Language-Like Communication without a Language Model," *Science*, 197:401–403.

Goodman, N. (1954), *Fact, Fiction, and Forecast*, University of London, Athlone Press.

Goodman, N. (1978), *Ways of Worldmaking*, Indianapolis, Hackett Publishing Co.

Gough, P., Alford, J., and Halley-Wilcox, P. (1978), "Words and Contexts," unpublished ms presented at the National Reading Conference, St. Petersburg Beach, Fla., November 1978.

Haber, R. (1980), "How We Remember What We See", in R. and R. Atkinson (eds.), *Mind and Behavior, Readings from Scientific American*, San Francisco, W. H. Freeman.

Hanson, N. (1958), *Patterns of Discovery*, Cambridge, England, Cambridge University Press.

Harris, J. (1977), "Leibniz and Locke on Innate Ideas," in I. C. Tipton (ed.), *Locke on Human Understanding*, Oxford Readings in Philosophy, Oxford University Press.

Haugeland, J. (1981), "Semantic Engines: An Introduction to Mind Design," in J. Haugeland (ed.), *Mind Design*, Vermont, Bradford Books.

Hollander, B. (1920), *In Search of the Soul*, New York, E. P. Dutton.

Hume, D. *Enquiries Concerning the Human Understanding and Concerning the Principles of Morals*, L. Selbey-Biggs (ed.), Oxford, Oxford University Press, in press.

Intraub, H. (1981), "Rapid Conceptual Identification of Sequentially Presented Pictures," *Journal of Experimental Psychology: Human Perception and Performance*, 7,3:604–610.

Kaplan, R., and Bresnan J. (1982), "Lexical Functional Grammar: A Formal System for Grammatical Representation," in J. Bresnan (ed.), *The Mental Representation of Grammatical Relations*, Cambridge, Mass., MIT Press.

Kintsch, W. (1974), *The Representation of Meaning in Memory*, New York, John Wiley and Sons.

Kline, D. (1970), *A History of Scientific Psychology*, New York, Basic Books.

Kosslyn, S. (1980), *Image and Mind*, Cambridge, Mass., Harvard University Press.

Kuhn, T. (1970), *The Structure of Scientific Revolutions*, 2d ed., Chicago, University of Chicago Press.

Lackner, J., and Garrett, M. (1973), "Resolving Ambiguity; Effects of Biasing Context in the Unattended Ear," *Cognition*, 1:359–372.

Lewis, J. (1970), "Semantic Processing of Unattended Messages Using Dichotic Listening," *Journal of Experimental Psychology*, 85:225–228.

Liberman, A., Cooper, F., Shankweiler, D., and Studdert-Kennedy, M. (1967), "The Perception of The Speech Code," *Psychological Review*, 74:431–461.

Lieberman, P. (1965), "On the Acoustic Basis of the Perception of Intonation by Linguists," *Word*, 21:40–54.

Locke, J. (1975), *An Essay Concerning Human Understanding*, P. Nidditch (ed.), Oxford at the Clarendon Press.

Loewenstein, W. (1960), "Biological Transducers, *Scientific American*, Also in *Perception: Mechanisms and Models: Readings from Scientific American* (1972), San Francisco, Freeman.

Macdonald, J., and McGurk, H. (1978), "Visual Influences on Speech Perception Processes," *Perception and Psychophysics*, 24:253–257.

Marcus, M. (1977), "A Theory of Syntactic Recognition for Natural Language," Ph.D. thesis, M.I.T.

Marr, D., and Nishihara, H. (1978), "Visual Information Processing: Artificial Intelligence and the Sensorium of Sight," *Technology Review*, October, 28–49.

Marr, D., and Poggio, T. (1977), "From Understanding Computation to Understanding Neural Circuitry," *Neurosciences Research Progress Bulletin*, 15:470-488.

Marshall, J. (1980), "The New Organology," *The Behavorial and Brain Sciences*, 3:23–25.

Marshall, J. (1981), "Cognition at the Crossroads," *Nature*, 289:613–614.

Marslen-Wilson, W. (1973), "Speech Shadowing and Speech Perception," Ph.D. thesis, M.I.T.

Marslen-Wilson, W., and Tyler, L. (1981), "Central Processes in Speech Understanding," *Philosophical Transactions of the Royal Society*, B 295:317–322.

Marslen-Wilson, W., and Tyler, L. (1982a), "Explanatory Models in Psycholinguistics," ms presented at the conference on Modelling Real-Time Language Processes, St Maximin, France.

Marslen-Wilson, W., and Tyler, L. (1982b), "Processing Utterances in Discourse Contexts: On-Line Resolution of Anaphors," ms, Max-Planck-Institut für Psycholinguistik, Nijmegen.

McCarthy, J. (1980), "Circumscription—A Form of Non-Monotonic Reasoning," *Artificial Intelligence*, 13:27–39.

McCarthy, J., and Hayes, P. (1969), "Some Philosophical Problems from the Standpoint of Artificial Intelligence," in B. Meltzer and D. Mitchie (eds.), *Machine Intelligence*, 4, New York, American Elsevier.

McGurk, H., and Macdonald, J. (1976), "Hearing Lips and Seeing Voices," *Nature*, 264:746–748.

Meltzoff, A., and Bonton, R. (1979), "Intermodal Matching," *Nature*, 282:403–404.

Meyer, D., and Schvanerveldt, R. (1971), "Facilitation in Recognizing Pairs of Words: Evidence of a Dependence between Retrieval Operations," *Journal of Experimental Psychology*, 90:227–234.

Miller, G. (1956), "The Magical Number Seven Plus or Minus Two," *Psychological Review*, 63:81–96.

Miller, G., Galanter, E., and Pribram, K. (1960), *Plans and the Structure of Behavior*, New York, Holt.

Miller, G., and Isard, S. (1963), "Some Perceptual Consequences of Linguistic Rules," *Journal of Verbal Learning and Verbal Behavior*, 2:217–228.

Milner, B., Corbin, S., and Teuber, H.-L. (1968), "Further Analysis of the Hippocampal Amnesic Syndrome: 14-Year Follow-Up Study of H. M.", *Neuropsychologia*, 6:215–234.

Minsky, M. (1975), "A Framework for Representing Knowledge," in P. Winston (ed.), *The Psychology of Computer Vision*, New York, McGraw Hill.

Morton, J. (1967), "A Singular Lack of Incidental Learning," *Nature*, 215:203–204.

Morton, J. (1969), "The Interaction of Information in Word Recognition,"*Psychological Review*, 76:165–178.

Nickerson, R., and Adams, M. (1979), "Long-Term Memory for a Common Object," *Cognitive Psychology*, 11:287–307.

Nisbett, R., and Ross, L. (1980), *Human Inference: Strategies and Shortcomings of Social Judgment*, Englewood Cliffs, N.J., Prentice-Hall.

Ortony, A. (ed.) (1979), *Metaphor and Thought*, Cambridge, England, Cambridge University Press.

Piatelli-Palimarini, M. (ed.) (1980), *Language and Learning: The Debate between Jean Piaget and Noam Chomsky*, Cambridge, Mass., Harvard University Press.

Pinker, S. (1979), "Formal Model of Language Learning" *Cognition*, 7,3:217–283.

Pisoni, D., and Tash, J. (1974), "Reaction Times to Comparisons within and across Phonetic Categories," *Perception and Psychophysics*, 15,2:285–290.

Plato, "Theatetus," F. M. Cornford (tr.), in E. Hamilton and H. Cairns (eds.), *Plato: The Collected Dialogues*, Princeton, N.J., Princeton University Press, 1963.

Plato, "Meno," W. Guthrie (tr.), in E. Hamilton and H. Cairns (eds.), *Plato: The Collected Dialogues*, Princeton, N.J., Princeton University Press, 1963.

Posner, M. *Chronometric Studies of Mind*, Hillsdale, N.J., Lawrence Erlbaum Associates, in press.

Potter, M. (1975), "Meaning in Visual Search," *Science*, 187: 965–966.

Putnam, H. (1961), "Some Issues in the Theory of Grammar," in R. Jakobsen (ed.), *Proceedings of the Twelfth Symposium of Applied Mathematics: Structure of Language and Its Mathematical Aspects*, Providence, R.I., American Mathematical Society.

Putnam, H. (1962), "The Analytic and the Synthetic" in H. Feigl and G. Maxwell (eds.), *Minnesota Studies in the Philosophy of Science*, III, Minneapolis, University of Minnesota Press.

Putnam, H. (1980), "What Is Innate and Why," in M. Piatelli-Palmarini (ed.), *Language and Learning, q.v.*.

Pylyshyn, Z. (1980), "Computation and Cognition: Issues in the Foundations of Cognitive Science," *Behavorial and Brain Sciences*, 3:111–132.

Pylyshyn, Z. (1981), "The Nativists Are Restless," *Contemporary Psychology*, 26,7:501–504.

Quine, W. (1953), "Two Dogmas of Empiricism," in *From a Logical Point of View*, Cambridge, Mass., Harvard University Press.

Raphael, B. (1971), "The Frame Problem in Problem-Solving Systems," in N. Findler and B. Metzler (eds.), *Artificial Intelligence and Heuristic Programming*, Edinburgh, Edinburgh University Press.

Rosch, E., Mervis, C., Gray, W., Johnson, D., and Boyes-Braem, P. (1976), "Basic Objects in Natural Categories," *Cognitive Psychology*, 8:382–439.

Rozin, P. (1976), "The Evolution of Intelligence And Access to the Cognitive Unconscious," in *Progress in Psychobiology and Physiological Psychology*, Vol. 6, New York, Academic Press.

Rorty, R. (1979), *Philosophy and the Mirror of Nature*, Princeton, Princeton University Press.

Sachs, J. (1967), "Recognition Memory for Syntactic and Semantic Aspects of Connected Discourse," *Perception and Psychophysics*, 2:437–442.

Samuel, A. (1981), "Phoneme Restoration: Insights from a New Methodology," *Journal of Experimental Psychology: General*, 110,4:474–494.

Schank, R., and Abelson, R. (1975), "Scripts, Plans and Knowledge," *Proceedings of the Fourth International Joint Conference on Artificial Intelligence*, Tbilisi. Republished in P. Johnson-Laird and P. Wason, *Thinking*, Cambridge, England, Cambridge University Press, 1977.

Spearman, C. (1927), *The Abilities of Man*, New York, Macmillan.

Spearman, C. (1930), *Psychology down the Ages* (2 vols.), London, Macmillan.

Spelke, E. (1982), "Perceptual Knowledge of Objects in Infancy," in J. Mehler, E. Walker, and M. Garret (eds.), *Perspectives on Mental Representation*, Hillsdale, N.J., N. Lawrence Erlbaum Associates.

Stampe, D. (1977), "Toward a Causal Theory of Linguistic Representation," *Midwest Studies in Philosophy*, 2:42–63.

Stich, S. (1978), "Beliefs and Subdoxastic States," *Philosophy of Science*, 45:499–518.

Stout, G. (1930), *Studies in Philosophy and Psychology*, London, Macmillan.

Swinney, D. (1979), "Lexical Access during Sentence Comprehension: (Re)consideration of Context Effects," *Journal of Verbal Learning and Verbal Behavior*, 18:645–660.

Takavolian, S. (ed.) (1981), *Language Acquisition and Linguistic Theory*, Cambridge, Mass., MIT Press.

Tannenhaus, M., Leiman, J., and Seidenberg, M. (1979), "Evidence for Multiple Stages in the Processing of Ambiguous Words in Syntactic Contexts," *Journal of Verbal Learning and Verbal Behavior*, 18:427–441.

Thagard, P. (1980), "Scientific Theories as Frame Systems," unpublished ms, University of Michigan, Dearborn.

Treisman, A., and Gelade, G. (1980), "A Feature-Integration Theory of Attention," *Cognitive Psychology*, 12:97–136.

Ullman, S. (1979), *The Interpretation of Visual Motion*, Cambridge, Mass., MIT Press.

Wanner, E. (1968), "On Remembering, Forgetting, and Understanding Sentences: A Study of the Deep Structure Hypothesis," Ph.D. thesis, Harvard University.

Warren, R. (1970), "Perceptual Restoration of Missing Speech Sounds," *Science*, 167:392–393.

Wright, B. (1982), "Syntactic Effects from Lexical Decision in Sentences: Implications for Human Parsing," Ph.D. thesis, M.I.T.

Yin, R. (1969), "Looking at Upside-Down Faces," *Journal of Experimental Psychology*, 81:141–145.

Yin, R. (1970), "Face Recognition by Brain Injured Patients: A Dissociable Ability?" *Neuropsychologia*, 8:395–402.

Zucker, S. (1981), "Computer Vision and Human Perception," Technical report 81-10, Computer Vision and Graphics Laboratory, McGill University.